THE INDIE AUTHOR BESTIARY

AN EPIC QUEST AGAINST THE BEASTS OF THE WRITING WORLD

M.L. RONN

WHAT YOU'LL LEARN IN THIS BOOK

You're probably thinking "what is a bestiary and what does it have to do with writing and self-publishing?"

I'll explain—but first, a history lesson.

According to Merriam-Webster, a bestiary is a medieval allegorical or moralizing work on the appearance and habits of real or imaginary animals.

In other words, a bestiary is a compendium of beasts. In medieval times, citizens used bestiaries to make sense of the natural world and to understand the glory of God. In seeing everyday creatures such as pelicans and snakes, they could associate the animals with a story in the Bible.

Take the story of the pelican. There's a famous story about a pelican mother whose birds begin to strike her with their beaks. In rage, the mother kills the children, but when she realizes what she's done, she tears a hole in her chest, releasing a torrent of blood, which washes over the children and revives them. This is a clear metaphor for the Christian God.

We can see in the bestiaries moral stories about the snake and how it tempted Eve in the Garden of Eden, or unicorns wandering through lonely forests, illusive to all in society except virgins, or the beaver, who ripped its testicles off and threw them at hunters (not kidding).

It is from the bestiary tradition that we revere the lion. Bestiaries often presented lions first and proclaimed them "the king of the beasts." The cover of this book bears a lion's head as a tribute to that tradition.

Bestiary manuscripts contained beautiful illustrations of the animals accompanied by a moral story, which provided guidance to the people of the time about how to live their lives. The manuscripts were translated into many languages too, and had international appeal.

Medieval bestiaries inspired modern-day equivalents. J.K. Rowling's *Fantastic Beasts and Where to Find Them* in the Harry Potter series is a great example. So is the Pokédex from the Pokémon series.

Today, the medium has evolved from a moral tool to a practical one.

Figuratively, *Fantastic Beasts* informs the wizards in the Harry Potter world of the ways of magical creatures and how to kill them; the Pokédex teaches Pokémon trainers the best ways to battle and catch wild Pokémon.

Literally, *Fantastic Beasts* was an additional stream of income for J.K. Rowling and a way to help immerse her readers in the lore of her world; the Pokédex has spawned countless books and apps about the world of Pokémon.

The bestiary format is a useful tool in many ways.

So, what about writers?

This book is not about helping you understand the glory of God, and it's not about medieval times. Rather, this book is a book of allegories.

Think about all the problems we face in the writing life: fear, self-doubt, hubris, and so much more. If you think about them, they have the characteristics of beasts—they're fearsome, ferocious, and deadly under the right circumstances. And what do you do with beasts?

First, you read a bestiary to understand their ways. Then you slay them.

The Indie Author Bestiary will help you slay the "beasts" of the writing world because there are many.

I've said for a while that one of the biggest problems that writers face is that their tools and problems are invisible.

What do we mean when we say "improve your writing craft?" What are you improving? You're honing a skill that is 100 percent mental. You can't touch it and you can't hold it. Instead, you must visualize it in your mind. I wrote a book called *The Indie Author Atlas* to help writers visualize the things they need to learn in the writing life because my belief is that if you can visualize something, you can learn it. My book *Mental Models for Writers* transforms breakthrough ideas in the world of mental models into practical tools so that you can use them to solve problems in your writing life. The book takes the invisible and makes it visible. This is true of all the aforementioned books too.

Self-doubt, fear, and hubris are common in a writer's life, but they're invisible foes. If you could see them and recognize them whenever they entered your life, you could arm yourself against them and protect yourself from their advances. Therefore, this bestiary can be useful to you. **This book makes the invisible beasts of the writing world visible and gives you the tools you need to destroy them.**

A Note About the Beastmaster

.   .   .

My name is M.L. Ronn. I have written over 50 books. My books are available in ebook, paperback, and audio, with some of the audio professionally narrated by me.

I became an author after a near-death experience made me realize that life is too short not to follow your dreams.

I host the popular YouTube channel Author Level Up, which has tens of thousands of subscribers who want to master the craft of writing. I've spoken to crowds of over 1,000 authors about writing and publishing. I built a writing career while raising a family, working a full-time job, and attending law school classes in the evening. At the time of this writing, I am also the Outreach Manager for the Alliance of Independent Authors (ALLi), a nonprofit association that assists self-published writers achieve their dreams.

I've experienced the many beasts of the writing world first-hand, and somehow I've lived to tell about it. My journey hasn't been without wounds; even though I'm a well-seasoned traveler and my weapons are sharp and ready, I still get ambushed sometimes. I have the scars to prove it. The beasts of this world are relentless, and they will use any opportunity to strike. You must always be on your guard.

The beasts of the writing world are responsible for many writer deaths each day. These beasts do not feed on blood, but careers; they do not hunger for bones, but for the complete destruction of everything you hold dear as a writer. Fire-breathing dragons have *nothing* on these beasts...

If I can keep you alive, dear writer, or at least help you avoid a few flesh wounds, then the few dollars you spent on this book will have been worth it.

But you're not ready to fight, yet. We must first make a trip to the arsenal so we can arm you for the journey ahead.

I'll be your guide. Stay alert and always be ready for a fight, for there are beasts in this world who mean us harm. Let's learn all about them, shall we?

. . .

M.L. Ronn
Des Moines, Iowa
September 2, 2020

THE ARSENAL: WEAPONS YOU'LL NEED

Welcome to the arsenal. Let's have a look around. And no, don't judge me because I have lots of weapons—an entire warehouse of them.

Don't you like the skylights? I think they make the swords on the west wall POP. I've accrued many of these weapons over the years—some from mentors, others that I've fashioned myself with a little bit of know-how. We'll get you suited up with the most important ones.

Yes, it's very American of me to speak so casually in terms of violence, but these aren't lions and tigers we're talking about. Animal rights activists aren't going to hunt you down for wounding self-doubt, you see. You won't go to jail for murdering magical thinking. So spare me.

I've been ambushed enough times out of the blue to know better, and once it happens to you a few times, I'm certain that you'll agree with my rhetoric. We're preparing you for war, and like any good soldier, you're going to need a few weapons.

YOUR FIRST WEAPON OF CHOICE: WORDS

. . .

Here you go. It's a sword imbued with the magical residue of words. Cold blue steel with a leather scabbard. It's heavier than it looks, isn't it? Hold it up to the light and you can see a message etched into the steel: "Words are the writer's best weapon."

Every time you sit down to write, this sword grows stronger. With every book you write, this sword doubles in strength. Even a beginning writer can wield a lot of power with this thing, as long as they keep writing.

Words are your best friend on this journey. The beasts of the writing world will try to stop you from achieving words. Words are your strength and momentum, and they come with perspective.

Whenever you face a beast, more often than not, the best thing to do is apply words to the situation. Fear hates the accumulation of word counts. The more words you write, the harder it will be for fear to stop you. Why do you think you can't spell s-w-o-r-d without the w-o-r-d? That's one of the divine secrets of the universe!

YOUR SECOND WEAPON OF CHOICE: ACTIONS

If words don't work against a beast, then your next best alternative is action.

Take action.

Beasts don't like to work hard for their food. They prefer to eat easier prey. They're used to writers seizing up in their presence so they can devour them whole. The writers slide right down, especially with a little barbecue sauce.

It's easy to freeze when you see a beast, but all it takes to stave them off is a single step...toward your goal. When you take action, you're signaling to them that they have no power over you. They can't stop you from doing what you want to do. That's unappealing to them.

Combine words with action and you'll be a formidable opponent.

YOUR SHIELD: KNOWLEDGE

I hate to give this shield away, but you're going to need it. It's heavy too, but the leather strap is easy to hold. It'll protect you, but most beasts can bust it after a few blows. It won't save you forever. I didn't want to give this shield to you because I love the book image painted on it. No beast likes the sight of that!

Beasts feed off ignorance. The less you know, the higher the likelihood of beasts appearing in your life.

If you don't know the ins and outs of writing and self-publishing, then you can't protect yourself against fraud, for example.

Therefore, you must always thirst for knowledge, for it is the lifeblood of a successful writer. Things like writing craft, business, and marketing aren't sexy to learn, but learning them is the *only* way you can reduce the appearance of beasts.

The writing world is full of writers who don't have knowledge to defend themselves upon the appearance of a beast. These writers are scammed by fraud. They fall for marketing techniques that don't work, and thus leave themselves open to the beasts of desperation and self-doubt. They refuse to learn and so grow stagnant and susceptible to one of the most vicious beasts of all—burnout.

All of this can be avoided if you pursue knowledge. Pursue it often and never tire of it. When you think you know it all, humble yourself and keep learning. Knowledge is beast repellent.

YOUR ARMOR: POSITIVE THINKING

Hold your arms up. Suck in your waist. There we go. I promise I'm not trying to be awkward. We've got to get measurements for your armor.

This armor is heavy too. When a beast slashes you for the first time, you'll thank me for it.

Ah! Here we go! This armor will fit you just fine. It's armor with shoulder plates and leather scale armor so you can move quickly. You'll like the heft it gives you in battle. Let's test it— run from here to the stained-glass window over there. Three, two, go—!

Looking good, my friend! You're not even out of breath. You'll be wearing this armor for life. You're going to be a muscular warrior in just a few weeks!

I see you're staring at the window. It's gorgeous, isn't it? I commissioned a local company to install a gothic stained-glass window with a typewriter on an emerald green hill surrounded by clouds, birds, and sun rays. On a clear, moonlit night, it spins a typewriter shadow onto the floor. If you kneel on it and look up through the skylight, you'll see the moon and feel the power of the written word enveloping you. Try it.

Good job. Can you feel it?

I forgot to tell you that this armor is forged with a thousand positive words. Words such as "abundance," "love," "fearless," "kindness," "respect," and "meditation" are etched on the back of each scale. The maker uttered these positive words over and over and listened to positive music as she stitched the armor together by hand. This armor was birthed by optimism. Just as the armor protects you from a beast's claws, it too will improve the power of your positive thinking. It will magnify your thoughts. A simple utterance to yourself that you are worth it will radiate throughout your armor. You won't be able to see it, but beasts will. Positive thinking is like holy water to them. At the same time, the light will attract other writers. Someone wrote once that when your love light shines, it makes the whole world brighter. Let that love light shine in everything you do. Not only will you improve your writing and your life, but you will also improve the world.

I'll give you a moment to soak in the moonlight. When you're ready, I'll see you in that enclave over there with the bookshelves and candles.

Let's go to my alchemy lab.

YOUR MAGIC POTION: TIME

Ignore the beakers and vials all over the place. I'm not too good at alchemy. I just dabble in it. I've never turned rocks into gold, but I have turned bad situations into good ones.

The only potion that has worked for me is this one—this green liquid in a bottle shaped like an hourglass. It's a liquid manifestation of time. Drink, let time pass as you zoom into the future, and you'll see problems in the writing world in a different perspective.

All potions have side effects, though. Drink too much of this and you'll disassociate with time. That's bad in the long-term. If you don't drink it at all, you'll lose sense of time in the short-term, tackling a problem over and over again and not realizing that you need to step back.

Sometimes the best remedy for a writer is time. Your manuscripts sometimes need time. Your books need time to find their readers. You need time to solve the problems you face. Your business needs time to generate profits. You get the picture.

Be careful when using this potion in the presence of beasts. Sometimes it will diminish a beast's power; other times, it will make the beast bigger. Some problems can't be solved with the passage of time. You'll learn this the hard way when you have to fight beasts that swell to three times their size after you drink the potion. In my experience, these beasts can always be slain, but you'll have to work harder. You'll accrue wisdom after you use the potion a few times.

The potion regenerates itself at reducing rates. It will replenish itself, but always a little less every time you use it. Near the end of your life, there won't be very much potion left. Let it be a reminder of how little time you have, even though it's a *lot* of time.

You're looking like a knight of the written word now, fellow writer! I've got one more gift for you, and then your knighting will be complete. Let's go outside.

YOUR DRAGON SUMMON: RESOURCEFULNESS

I bet the last thing you expected to see was a dragon!

Meet your new companion. It stands ready to fight with you. It's a fourteen-foot-tall, spiky-scaled, fire-breathing, jewel-eyed dragon fighter!

I'll give you two a moment. You can customize the dragon: just ask and it will change its scale color and body type to suit your personality.

Pretty cool, huh? Imagine the look on beasts' faces when your dragon descends from the clouds to make some barbecue!

Your dragon will help you from time to time. Use it too much and you'll burn yourself out in the dragon's flames.

The best time to summon your dragon is when you can't seem to find a way to slay a beast. The beasts will retreat upon hearing your dragon roar; the clouds will part, and it will swoop down, engulfing the battlefield in fire, giving you time to retreat and clear your mind.

The dragon represents resourcefulness. We all have times when we are cornered and no solution seems to be working. Call your dragon's name, watch the hellfire, and when the flames subside, study the landscape and prepare a new mode of attack.

A WORD WARRIOR IS BORN

You will do battle with:

- A **sword** imbued with the magical residue of words,
- **actions** that move your writing life forward,
- a **shield** of knowledge,
- **armor** forged with positive thinking and optimism,
- a **magic potion** of time, and
- a **dragon** who will give you resourcefulness and second wind in the face of true adversity.

It's time to journey into the writing world and do battle, my fellow writer. When we reach the end of this book, you'll know how to slay the major beasts.

WAIT, WHAT'S THAT SOUND???

The dragon is roaring. It doesn't do that unless—get down!

The earth hasn't shaken like this since I embarked on my journey as a writer and...

Look to the east!

Stand, my fellow writer. Destiny calls us. Dragon, take us to the sky!

Hold on tight. I need to show you something. We're rising now—a little higher, dragon!—there. Do you see it? The giant stone tower rising from the darkest depths of the jewel-dark sea?

The beasts have heard our preparations and are responding in kind. They mean to destroy us now. The tower is many stories high. It may well claw at the gates of heaven!

I knew this day would come, but I didn't think it would be today.

Dragon, look out!

Whew...that was a spell blast from the tower. Do you hear the beast's chanting on the wind?

My fellow writer, the tower is calling its sinspawn home. In just a few hours, every beast in the writing world will be in the tower, growling our names.

The tower challenges us to war, to storm its dark dungeon, and fight our way to the top.

I have been waiting for this day for years. Now might be the time I get my rematch.

As a young knight, I stormed this very tower, but the beasts were too powerful. I made it halfway up the tower, but I misjudged a battle with the beast of self-doubt. I was no match for it. I should have died, but my armor saved me from the beast's final slash.

It threw me into the sea. I'll never forget the beast's laughter as I plummeted into the cold water. And its...its face of fire, gnashing teeth and seven mouths—each one cursing me in different tones of my own voice! I prayed that the fall would put me out of my misery once and for all—but no, dear writer. This life had bigger plans for me, for I survived.

I drifted for days on the waves under a gunmetal sky, nearly perishing until I washed up on the shore of a deserted island. An old man and his wife lived there in a little hut on the beach. They too were word warriors defeated at the tower. I spent seven years on the island under their tutelage, learning about their glorious but ill-fated quest. In their lessons, I learned the errors of my ways.

One morning, I awoke early to have a writing session on the beach. When I returned to the hut, I discovered the couple had both died in their sleep. I cried over their bodies for three days—I could not contain my sadness and rage, for I did not want to leave the island, but the couple had always told me that I would have to one day. I wasn't ready.

I buried them on the beach on that hot, hot morning, the sea spray lashing my back and vultures circling overhead. It was time for me to begin my journey again. I fashioned a raft from driftwood.

When I returned to the couple's hut to pay my final respects to the place where I learned to become a true writer, I took the couple's journal of secret writer techniques. I have carried that journal with me over the decades. It has taken me that long to truly learn its lessons.

I drifted on the ocean for many years until I landed on the shores of this town. I built this arsenal behind my home so that I could pay my learning forward to other writers. Now is the time I must avenge my mentors and redeem myself. (And help you too!)

The tower calls us, my fellow writer. We must rise to meet this moment, for it may be the last one we get.

Dragon, take us down.

Allow me to suit up and call my dragon. I will ride with you and we will fight side-by-side. Together we will take the tower!

THE TOWER OF LAUGHING BEASTS

Dragons, stay the course over the ocean. The tower is looming near.

How are you feeling, fellow writer? It's okay to be nervous. Channel your thoughts into positive ones. It'll steady your nerves. Don't look down at the water—there are sharks.

A storm is moving in from the west. We'll be ascending the tower in the middle of a storm, with a soundtrack of thunder, sword clinks, and beastly howls.

The tower is bigger than it looked from afar. Clouds shroud its top. We're in for a battle of endurance.

Dragons, land on the beach there.

I wish that we had more time to train you. I will forever cherish the short time we spent in the arsenal. However, one never can train enough—we're almost always thrown into battle against our will. An aspiring writer is *never* ready for their first battle. If they were, there would be a lot more successful writers.

Keep your hand on your hilt at all times.

Thank you, dragons. Take to the skies again and stay near, for we will need you. Be safe, friends!

I know what you must be feeling, fellow writer. Your nerves still aren't steady, and that's okay. This beach is the place where your career will be made. There's no turning back now. If you don't want to continue, wade into the waves; the sharks will be glad to have a meal.

You're not turning back? That's exactly what I want to hear.

Let us take a look at our tower now.

The gate is a few yards away—a massive brown door with a lion knocker. That door leads into the torchlit coliseum on the first floor. We must fight our first battle among the bones of writers.

Are you ready, fellow writer? Then lift the knocker and rap seven times. Put all your force into it. I'll wait here with my sword drawn.

Wham.

Wham.

Wham.

Wham.

Wham.

Wham. WHAM!

Get back, fellow writer! Sword at the ready! Duck. Duck!!

That was close. That purple tentacle nearly grabbed you. It retreated into the darkness.

Did you hear that ghastly scream? Our first beast beckons us.

BEAST #1: FEAR

This coliseum is exactly as I remember it: the smell of mold, mortar, and death; the ocean waves raging against the walls; clerestory windows letting in gray moonbeams slanting down to an oval field of sand. The sand is black from the blood spilled from writers.

Beware the grates in the walls. The beast's tentacles emerge from there.

We'll stand in the middle of the coliseum and invoke the beast's name.

The walls are shaking now. The grates have become unmoored, and now its tentacles have crawled out. Purple and slimy, full of suckers. They slither in a strange dance along the walls.

Take note, my fellow writer—there are three tentacles. Keep an eye on all of them and never lose their location.

It's raising its first tentacle to strike. En garde!

THE FIRST TENTACLE: ANTI-CREATIVITY

. . .

"Why are you writing? The world would benefit more if you took up a trade."

Don't listen to the beast's ghastly voice. It's trying to dissuade you from being a writer.

"No one will want read your work. You're a beginner. You're not good enough."

Cut the tentacle. Don't think about it.

SLASH!

Good job! That slash was worth at least 2000 words. Keep slashing!

Oh no—you've taken a hit. Get up and say the following affirmations with me as you continue your slashes.

I will finish my book.

No one will stop me.

Readers want my book, and I must give it to them.

I will be successful.

Way to go, fellow writer—your slashes were worth 50,000 words, or one full-length novel.

The stump is writhing. Finish it off.

Writer, six o'clock!

THE SECOND TENTACLE: ANTI-FINISHING

"This book isn't good enough. I need to rewrite it."

Writer, this tentacle is more devious. Words won't work. Arm yourself with positive thinking and repeat after me.

I am the worst judge of my work. Only readers decide whether my work is good.

"But how can you know if your book is good when you've never done this before? Compare it to a mega bestseller and see how good you are."

I may not be perfect, but I'm a work in progress. The only way to progress is to keep writing NEW books. I won't let you trap me in the theater of my mind.

Fear didn't like that one. The beast is wailing now. This is our chance. Advance toward the tentacle and say the date that you're going to finish your novel, and your first step toward finishing your drafts.

Yes! You've embraced the power of action.

The tentacle couldn't handle it—it's withered to half its size now and sliding back into the grate.

THE THIRD TENTACLE: ANTI-MARKETING AND ANTI-BUSINESS

"This book is a failure. No one is buying it. Perhaps I should rewrite it."

We'll have to finish it off—but we must summon our dragons and retreat, for we'll need a different plan of attack.

They've flown in through the windows and are spraying fire across the coliseum.

Let's retreat from the flames, fellow writer!

How might we end this tentacle's hold on us?

The reality is that we will find ourselves in this situation many times where our books aren't selling. We'll want them to sell because we may want to escape our lousy jobs, or pay off our debt, or pursue real happiness. And yet, the writing income just can't provide that for us. Not with the speed we desire.

The answer that most don't want to hear is to keep pushing. Keep writing, keep failing, keep finding new readers, keep trying new things in your writing business. Most writers succumb to this tentacle because they can't handle this truth. But we can.

As the dragons lay their final hellfire on the beast, let us say the finishing blow.

I know my why. I know exactly why I am doing this. I know exactly why I am here, and I'm in this for the long haul.

Done. The tentacle exploded into dust. Thank you, dragons. Be safe!

Fellow writer, that model combined with eternal optimism was poison to this beast.

We've defeated the third and final tentacle. Now you'll finally see the true face of this beast.

Fellow writer, hold your breath. The floor has dropped and we're falling toward into cold, dark water, and a giant maw is rising to meet us—! A tentacle's got me. You're on your own, my friend!

SPLASH!

THE BEAST'S MAW: YOUR FEELINGS OF SELF-WORTH

You hit the cold water and for a moment, all you can see is a wall of black and bubbles.

You ready your sword as you descend down, down.

Suddenly, something seizes you around your waist and constricts you, threatening to squeeze the oxygen left in your lungs. A tentacle. It drags you deeper into the ocean depths. The moonlight shining on the surface of the water is but a small ray now.

Something below catches your eye. Two yellow pinwheels of light appear far below, quickly rising.

As they move closer, you see that the pinwheels are the creature's eyes—two malformed, asymmetrical bloodshot eyes with no pupils. A mouth full of gleaming white teeth smiles, and opens wide.

In the dim light, you see Michael struggling in another tentacle next to you. There's nothing you can do to help him.

You can't slash the beast. You can't utter actions. You can't think of a spell.

Your grab the pouch on your belt for your last resort…you pull the hour-glass potion bottle, screw off the cap, and hurl it into the beast's mouth. It bounces off a tooth before disappearing down the beast's throat.

The beast stops and its mouth closes. Its eyes narrow.

The tentacles let you go.

You look to Michael, who is just as surprised as you. He motions to swim upward. You stroke upward to the gray moonbeams falling on the surface of the water.

You swim like you've never swam before, only looking back occasionally to see the beast in a contemplative gaze.

You're almost there…

Something grabs your leg. A tentacle!

It pulls you down, down…You're losing your air. Perhaps it would be better to resign yourself to fate. You'll never feel it when the beast devours you. All of a sudden, the water feels warm as the moonbeams drift further away…

SLASH!

Michael slashes the tentacle's tip off, freeing you. Below, the beast is grinning as it begins its ascent.

Michael grabs you and you give it one final burst of energy.

You tell yourself: *I can do it, I can do it, I can do it…*

You break through the surface of the water just in time, and oxygen rushes into your lungs. The next thing you hear is Michael's panting voice.

· · ·

THE FINAL BATTLE

We did it, fellow writer! That was close. But you took a big risk feeding that time potion to the beast. We'll see in a few moments if it worked.

The beast has broken through the water. Its head is exactly as I remember—a sickly purplish squid head with blisters all over. Its roar is deafening, and its breath—oh, my lord, does this thing need a breath mint or two! Seaweed, bowels, and rotting flesh!

It's not happy, fellow writer. Sword at the ready.

The beast is now growing to twice its size! It's growing and growing...we have a problem now.

The time potion must have allowed it to see forward into your life; it appears, my fellow writer, that you will suffer from fear for much of your life. Otherwise, it wouldn't have swelled to twice its size. It's emboldened.

That's helpful knowledge for us, but even more helpful for the beast, for he now knows your triggers.

I suppose you could slash me with your sword and end me now, for I have harmed you greatly. For that, you have my utmost apologies. However, I also consider myself a purveyor of inconvenient truths! But for my potion, you would have never survived against this beast. So now we must accept our circumstances and fight!

I will take it from the rear.

Damn. Its tentacles are regenerating.

Let us attack it with our full force, fellow writer!

Slash!

Slash!

Keep those words flowing!

A little help from our dragons, and we may be able to

charge the head. Yes, dragons, distract the deathly head of fear for us with your flames.

Fellow writer, jump high and aim for its left eye. I'll aim for the other one. Three, two, go!

There, we've blinded fear. It can't see us anymore. We'll slash off its last tentacle and that will finish it.

Tentacle gone. Good work. The beast is cowering now. We'll watch it die and then celebrate our first victory.

No, it isn't dying. It is retreating into the water. Do you hear its final warning?

"I'll have my revenge..."

Its tentacles are regenerating again, but they're disappearing into the grates.

Fellow writer, fear will be back. We'll have to stay on our guard. In the meantime, victory is ours and we may proceed to the next level of the tower. We'll take that staircase over there.

But first, let's debrief about our battle.

Remember when I told you that I carry my mentor's journal with me? I'd like to share a page from the book with you.

A MEDITATION FOR FEAR

Fighting fear means to do battle with a vicious beast in a coliseum where no one is watching.

To battle fear is to battle in the darkness. No one will know you're fighting it, and no one will care.

Fear is a many-tentacled creature who will meddle in every area of your writing life. Fear is anti-creativity and loves to see you give up on your stories. It is anti-production and loves to see you revise your books to oblivion and never even publish them. It is also anti-business and anti-marketing, sowing seeds of doubt that will make you question everything.

When you confront fear, you inform it that you know its ways. This makes the beast more dangerous, for it will try to drown you in your own doubt. It will wait patiently until you die in the darkness, and then it will devour you to make sure you're gone.

Fear is the only beast who knows you better than you know yourself. It was with you from the moment you were born, like a parasitic bacteria waiting for a moment to announce its presence.

It has been with you every day of your life, and it will be with you every day in the future. It never dies; only evolves. You can never kill fear; to kill fear is to kill yourself. But you must learn to live with it.

Learn to sense those pangs of doubt. The beast has learned to sow doubt in a way that is self-soothing.

"I can't..."

"I'll never..."

"No one will..."

These are the words of fear. The moment you think them and act upon them, you'll backslide.

Stay vigilant and be ruthless to the beast. Don't reason with it; force is the only language it understands.

BEAST #2: THE INFERIORITY COMPLEX

Fellow writer, do you hear that? It sounds like swordplay.

Ahead, there is a moonlit room in shambles. Curtains blow wildly around a crater in the wall overlooking the raging sea. And there is a knight in the room, swinging a sword wildly at our next beast. The knight is wearing a thick visor.

The Inferiority Complex hasn't changed. It's a nine-foot-tall gelatinous, human-shaped monstrosity. See how it raises its gooey arms—it leans to one side. Its legs drip into a pile of goop on the floor. It glows green, and its face is but a mass of hollow orifices—pinholes of light for eyes, and a toothless mouth. Our fellow knight isn't having any mercy on it, and neither should we. Let us assist our comrade!

Dear knight, we will be of assistance!

"I don't need any help! This beast is almost finished."

WHAM!

We distracted our friend to his detriment. He is hanging out the window now, and if I don't save him, he will plunge into the sea. Take his place, fellow writer!

. . .

THE BEAST

The beast roars as you draw your sword. It swings its arms like pendulums, cocking its head at you. Then you notice the slash marks across its chest.

Is that...blood dripping from its wounds? The beast is barely breathing. Has the knight nearly finished it off? The thought gives you confidence.

It throws a long punch at you, its arm extending like a javelin. You slash.

The arm splashes to the ground and burns the concrete. You kick the beast in the chest, knocking it down. It holds up its other arm, begging you for mercy.

You remember Michael's words. Show these beasts no mercy. Never appeal to their better nature, because they don't have one. You scream and raise your sword. You drive it into the beast's throat and show it that your actions are lethal. A muffled cry comes out as the beast bursts into green blossoms of goop. The walls are covered in it now. You're covered in it, and it stinks.

You sheathe your sword, scrunching your nostrils at the beast's fetid smell. But you'd rather smell death and despair than be dead yourself.

Metal footsteps track across the ground behind you, and you turn just in time to hear Michael yell.

You leap out of the way as the knight slashes in your direction.

Now it's Michael who is hanging out the window.

"Look out, fellow writer!" Michael cries.

"You robbed me of a kill," the knight says as you clash. "If it weren't for me, you wouldn't have been able to handle that beast."

"Don't listen to him," Michael says. "His words are toxic."

"But for me, you'd be nowhere. It was I who brought the beast to its final state, you worthless scoundrel."

Is he right? Did you claim an easy victory? Could this beast have destroyed you instead? Your mind fills with doubt.

The knight leaps at you, but you block his assault with your shield. The shield radiates with energy, knocking the knight into the wall.

"Fellow writer, listen to your shield's response," Michael says, finally climbing to safety and drawing his sword. "Listen to it and verbalize what it tells you."

You feel strange energy buzzing through your body.

As if possessed, you walk toward the knight, uttering a statement.

A MEDITATION FOR THE INFERIORITY COMPLEX

I am adequate. I am enough.

No one makes me feel inferior without my consent.

Just because the things I create may not have immediate value doesn't mean *I* don't have value.

There are things in this world that others do better than me, but that doesn't mean they are *better* than me.

I am the way I am because I prefer to be hard on myself, but kind to others.

The writing life makes me vulnerable to my emotions, but I vow to control them because it is the only thing standing between me and the control of my life.

The inferior complex has no hold on me. I will not reside in its wallowing.

. . .

THE BATTLE NEXT TIME

Fellow writer, your words have driven off the knight. He escaped up that staircase, which unfortunately happens to be our next destination.

I was a fool to think that helping that knight was wise. We'll see him again, but we can rejoice and fight the next beast.

Your recitation was similar to the notes in my journal. Well done. I'm impressed you could do that with no training!

Let us remember that our souls know the answers to the problems that we face, but that we inconveniently forget those answers! We must draw inner strength in the face of the inferiority complex. It takes courage to write a book, but it takes real courage to stand up to your inferiority complex.

BEAST #3: IMPOSTER SYNDROME

Now we come to a labyrinth of mirrors with tattered royal flags hanging from the rafters. I don't know about you, but I'm inclined not to look too hard at my reflection. You never know what you may see.

Quiet, fellow writer. I hear footsteps. It's probably our evil knight stalking around the place.

Indeed, there is his voice.

"Show yourself, you stupid beast!"

He's breaking mirrors now.

Behind you, fellow writer. There is our enemy's mark. A faceless, swirling apparition in the mirror behind you.

Ah, now it multiplies. There are apparitions all around us now.

Let us watch our blind fool teach us what we need to know about defeating this beast.

"Come out, come out, come out! Aaaaagh!"

The mirrors in the room are descending into the stone floor. The room is empty but for us and our friend. He looks exhausted.

"You won't slay my beast this time!"

We'll see about that, sir.

There is the apparition again, in front of a new staircase. The evil knight is rushing it—a trap door has opened beneath him. He has fallen into the darkness.

Even though he meant us harm, I will say a prayer for him. He will never climb from that hole.

The mirrors are rising again. The labyrinth is restored. Our true test begins.

We will walk the length of the labyrinth, for this beast can do us no harm. We'll have to have patience as we negotiate these mirrors, but it won't be too hard.

There. We've reached the staircase. The mirrors are descending again. Our apparition greets us now. Let us walk through it.

Hear that moaning? Our beast is dying, fellow writer. The apparition swirls on the floor, and a hand reaches up for us. We won't touch it. We'll let it writhe in its own pity and despair.

You see, fellow writer, the beast was the essence of the room, not anything in the room itself. The very notion of imposter syndrome is an illusion. We saved ourselves a major headache. Onward.

A MEDITATION FOR IMPOSTER SYNDROME

In the martial art of jujutsu, the goal is to disarm your opponent by using their own force against them. You should take the same approach with imposter syndrome.

This beast makes you feel as if you are in a room of mirrors. You think that you must find the correct version of the illusion, the version of yourself that will fit in with social circles, write better, and make you happier, but it is a sham.

Resist the initial urge to destroy your imposter or minimize its power. That is what the imposter wants. It wants you to break your hall of mirrors. In doing so, you harm yourself while the imposter goes unpunished.

The imposter is not in the room. The imposter *is* the room, and it seeks to suffocate everyone in it. If you feel like an imposter, chances are that everyone in the room also feels the same way.

The easier way to destroy your imposter is to leave the room. When you do, the beast will die, deprived of its food source.

In the end, you will find that the imposter was not an imposter at all, but a snapshot of your true self, which is never an easy thing to see. But your true self belongs in this world, and it fits in everywhere you go.

BEAST #4: TRAUMA

Fellow writer, there's a swirling portal at the top of the stairs.

It's mesmerizing, like a spinning blue galaxy in rapid motion.

You have no choice but to enter.

To where does it go, you ask?

To our most painful memories. I'll never forget my first time through this portal. Now it pains me to tell you that you must endure the same struggle.

See, fellow writer? I stepped right through the portal as if it were nothing. This beast has no sway on me.

When you step through, you're on your own.

But first, tell me—what are your "holes in the soul?" What dark secrets would you kill not to have revealed to the world? That is what you will deal with, my friend. My advice: address your fears head-on.

Good luck, fellow writer, and I pray we'll reunite soon!

INTO THE VORTEX

. . .

You leap into the portal, and it stretches you like yarn. You blaze through a blue tunnel. Wispy blue light pulses around you. The light is stuck on a black background as if scribbled into existence.

You hear voices beyond the blue. Kids. People talking. Like sound recordings, they have a warm, grainy texture to them. Just when you think you can identify some of the voices, they fade away.

You're flying faster through the tunnel now—if you smashed into something, you would die instantly. The tunnel snakes and swirls, the blue light becomes even more erratic, with the scribbled lines dancing to an irregular beat.

A corona of light temporarily blinds you before everything gives way to blackness.

You're floating in a fetal position.

Which way is up? You've lost your sense of orientation.

A deep, stentorian voice startles you.

"You dare to challenge me."

Before you is a giant mouth with square, yellowed teeth with a sagging gum line. Thick pink lips snarl at you. You detect the faint outline of a square chin in the darkness.

The head is at least size of a house. Everything from the nose up is shrouded in shadow.

"It's always a knight," the mouth says, grinning.

Fear burns your skin like a hot lamp. You couldn't attack this creature even if you wanted to.

"Go back to where you came from," the beast says.

A blue portal flashes behind you. Through it, you see Michael in the distance, straining to see inside. Can he see you?

Something tells you to draw your sword.

The beast laughs. The darkness swallows the echoes.

"You stupid knight," the head says. "You're outnumbered."

Then you feel the presence in the darkness grow—more

heads surround you on both sides now. The only way out is behind you.

What was it that Michael said before you entered?

My advice: address your fears head-on.

"Leave!" the heads shout at the same time. "Or we will crush you!"

You don't move.

The heads growl.

"If you don't turn around right now, we will show you ruthless violence like you've never seen."

Silence.

The heads roar again.

"This is your last chance, you stupid knight!" the heads say. "We will feast on your blood. Your armor is nothing to us."

You ready your sword.

"Leave, now!" the heads cry.

You tell them you're ready for a fight.

"We will fight you and destroy you!" the heads shout. They sound desperate.

They don't want a fight. You sense it. They want you to leave. If they wanted a fight, they could have destroyed you by now. Why haven't they?

You discover that you can swim through the darkness. You stroke toward the head in front of you.

"No!" the heads cry. "Turn around or you will die!"

You keep swimming and the beasts keep screaming. They sound like terrified animals now, their screams escalating into squeals.

My advice: address your fears head-on.

The heads scream and scream and scream as you swim right through the center head's hot mouth. You stab the back of the throat. The beast howls and a rush of air sucks you down its throat into deep darkness...

. . .

A CHAT WITH TRAUMA

The darkness burns away like paper set on fire. Shadow edges curl away to reveal a memory.

You know this memory.

It is a time when something in your life imploded—a time in your life that forever left a hole in your soul.

You know what it is. You know where it was. You remember how you felt.

You are there again, watching the painful event unfold. The emotions you felt rush back again, more vivid than the first time you felt them, and you have these pangs as you watch it, as if you could intervene and change it.

But you can't.

You can only watch as you relive your life in real-time.

The memory fades away to darkness, and the only thing you can think is "I feel..."

What do you feel?

Only you can answer that.

You begin to rise upward in the darkness. Suddenly, the top of the head's throat appears. The head's tongue is slanted to the side, its mouth open wide. The lips aren't moving.

You fear that the teeth will crush you as you fly out of the head, but they don't.

You look at the head. It is dead. It hangs to the side.

The other heads are dead too.

There is nowhere else to go but through the portal.

As you blaze back through the blue tunnel, you reflect on your feelings from the memory you saw. For the first time, you feel truly at peace about it.

Michael greets you as you exit the portal.

.   .   .

BACK TO REALITY

Fellow writer, you did it!

You are a good listener. My advice was perhaps cryptic, but you understood what I meant about attacking trauma head on. It's a fast-talking, scary beast, isn't it? But it has no power over you.

Catch your breath and let's head up that staircase over there.

A MEDITATION FOR TRAUMA

Trauma is something that happened to you, not something that is happening currently.

Fighting trauma is not intuitive. It is easier to run, yet the more you run, the more power it has over you.

Experiencing trauma initially is like being poisoned in small doses. The more you run, the more potent the poison becomes. One day, it builds up enough in your system that your body reacts negatively. It never ends well.

Therefore, your best action is to face trauma. Speak to it in the shaded darkness of your mind. It won't show its face to you, and it will scream and yell for you to go away. But when you confront it, it is powerless. It will die easily.

BEAST #5: BURNOUT

Do you feel that breeze, fellow writer? And the rain!

A wall has been destroyed. It's hard telling what this room was. Anything that was here has been blown through the crater in the wall.

Ah, here is our beast. It is materializing before us now in a blaze of orange.

It is a human in a slick leather jacket with a flaming head. His head is aflame. He's sitting on a motorcycle. He's waving his hands now—ah, two twin race tracks made from shining tiles are tracing themselves over the sea.

A motorcycle has appeared for us, fellow writer. This is one sick motorcycle, with giant exhaust pipes that remind me of a church organ. The beast is pointing to us now. He's challenging us to a race.

Me? I'm not driving that thing!

Let us ride our beast's motorcycle. We'll devise a winning strategy. We'll pretend to play his game, and then we'll let him win. Trust me on this.

You're revving that motorcycle like a pro, fellow writer! I'm going to be holding on to you for dear life. I have so much more to live for, fellow writer, so don't screw this up!

The beast is counting down now.

Three, two, one—let's ride!

We're traveling at the same speed. Don't look down, fellow writer—the waves are treacherous. Thank goodness we're wearing armor or the rain would be unbearable. What worries me is the lightning.

The beast is pulling ahead. Gun it!

We're past him now. Be careful with the loop. Don't lose control. Nice job navigating it.

We're circling each other far out over the ocean now—the tower is a distant speck now.

The beast just activated turbo thrusters on his motorcycle. He's way ahead of us now.

Hit that button on the handle.

Whoooooooa!!!!

We're caught up. The beast doesn't like that. He keeps looking over at us.

Another loop—phew, that one was scary.

The finish line is coming up. I can hear the beast laughing over the exhaust—he's going to pull a dirty trick. We'll let him.

See that other button on the handle? It's another turbo thruster. Hit it!

We're zooming ahead!

The beast just activated his second thruster as well. I can't believe how fast we're traveling, fellow writer!

Now hit the button again. Cut the thruster. Start applying your brakes, but not too hard. We don't want to slip into the sea.

Slow and steady, slow and steady, slow and steady. Watch out for those holes over there. If we had hit one of those holes at top speed, we would have died instantly. That was the trap.

The beast has crossed the finish line.

We have lost the race, fellow writer.

The beast awaits us at the finish line. When we cross, he will be done for.

Boom! His entire body is erupting into flames now! We didn't fall for his trick.

The racetrack is beginning to crumble. Let's get back to the tower, posthaste!

Excellent work, fellow writer. Let's push that damned motorcycle into the sea. Hopefully, we never see it again.

The racetrack has collapsed into the ocean as if it never existed. Our next staircase has appeared over there.

Onward!

A MEDITATION FOR BURNOUT

Burnout is a beast that challenges us to the most high-stakes race of all time. It loves to ride, ride, ride.

We feel as if we must return the mood in kind, and so we race.

But you can never beat burnout because the racetrack is rigged in its favor. It pushes you to ride faster and faster, even though it knows you'll never win. All it takes is one mistake to explode into flames or fly off the racetrack. That's exactly what burnout wants.

To play the game, understand your instinct to achieve. That in and of itself is a good thing, but when you find yourself ratcheting up your speed, remember to slow down, for there are holes in the racetrack, and when you hit one, you will cause misery and pain for yourself.

Burnout is the feeling that you can't move yourself to write. Writing suddenly has no joy. It feels like a burden. It pains you to think about it. This is a feeling that no writer should ever have to experience, and it is preventable.

Always write what motivates you. Don't do anything you don't want to do. Have fun. Always let burnout win the race. What do you truly lose if society laps you a few times? It'll have a phony race trophy, but you'll have your dignity and a long-term author career.

BEAST #6: WRITER'S BLOCK

We now move into a futuristic room. See the pulsing green lines on the floor and the wall? This place looks like something from a science fiction movie.

A giant cube hangs from the ceiling, connected to three wires. It hasn't changed one bit since I saw it—shimmering gold. It must be the size of a school bus.

A face is stirring in the cube. A nose, eyes, and a mouth are settling into place, the contours shifting like iron filings. The face looks trapped.

Sword and shield ready, fellow writer! The beast speaks.

"I have a three-question quiz for you."

Its voice is like a computer—stilted and electronic. It doesn't match the human-like face. Don't let it catch you off-guard. One of the wires suspending the beast is glowing—that's our true target.

"First question. Why can't I write? I sit down every day and try to concentrate, but the words just won't come. Tell me, knights, what the cause of my problem must be!"

The cube is counting down from twenty. We must summon

our dragons, fellow writer, for we will perish if we don't respond with the correct answer.

I hope our dragons can make it in time, for its question is a trap. It cannot concentrate because it has no ideas. We must show it resourcefulness.

This beast cannot be slain because it is artificial. It does not truly live, and therefore, it does not truly exist except for what we can see. That is the great trick to writer's block. If we accept its artificiality and turn the beast's energy upon itself, we can quickly eliminate it.

Here are the dragons, and just in time too, because the block has just stopped counting down. It's opening its eyes again.

"Now that's something I haven't seen in a long time. Those dragons inspire me. You have amused me, knights! I feel as if the fog is lifting…"

It's smiling. It's in such a state of delight that it won't mind if we slash that glowing cable up there. Fellow writer, get on your dragon and cut it. There! Come back down and let us prepare for the next question. The middle cable is glowing now.

The words on the wall have stopped appearing. The beast has a confused look on its face now.

"Second question. Your dragons inspired me, and it worked for a time. But now the words won't come again. What is stopping me?"

Allow me to assist you, fellow writer. I'll whisper in your ear. Ask it what it fears.

"I suppose…I fear that I cannot live up to my programming. The world can't accept a block like me."

There is our answer, fellow writer. Ask him if his thoughts are a result of his programming. Maybe he needs to reprogram himself!

"I've never considered that. Are you saying I'm faulty?"

No, not faulty, fellow writer. But normal! We all need reprogramming from time to time. Tell him about a time when you overcame negative thoughts.

"Perhaps fear is a bigger problem than I realize. You're right. I can do this. There's nothing stopping me from writing this book! I'm going to do it, knights. I am!"

It's smiling again. Words are appearing on the wall again— our beast is continuing its great novel again. Fly up and cut the middle cord. There!

The words have stopped. The beast is frowning again.

"Third question. Tell me, knights—you've given me courage, but now I still can't write. Why am I so stuck?"

Fellow writer, our beast has a bigger problem. It hangs from one wire, and all it will take to destroy it is one more slash. The cut wires are sparking. Our beast is in bad shape. We'll have to be cruel, but then again, we're playing a cruel game, aren't we? Tell him that two of his wires are snapped and that is the cause of his misfortune. If it'll simply close its eyes, we'll perform the necessary maintenance on it…

"My wires are damaged? Yes, of course, knights. You've given me resourcefulness and courage, so I trust you to finally end my writer's block."

It's smiling. Go, fellow writer! There we go.

The cube has fallen to the ground and shattered into many pieces. We've conquered writer's block.

Don't feel too bad about lying to him. Let's review our meditation to learn why.

A MEDITATION FOR WRITER'S BLOCK

Writer's block has three root causes.

The first cause is lack of inspiration. When you sit down at the keyboard and the words won't come, it may be because you need to fill your creative well. Reading often, consuming other media such as movies and television, and exposing yourself to new places, people, and perspectives will solve this problem in the short- and long-term.

The second cause is fear. We fall prey to the movies in our head about why we can't achieve our goals. The only way to beat fear is to keep moving forward and challenge the assumptions you hold about yourself. If you hear yourself say that you can't write a book because it's too hard, write the book anyway. You may be surprised at what happens. If you write the book, fear will retreat. If you fail, at least you tried. Fear is often always wrong.

Writers are so scared of fear. It dissuades us from doing many good things in our lives. But the secret to fear is that there are two types of fear. The first type of fear is ancestral fear; it's the warning bells that sound whenever you're in the presence of real danger. Our ancestors relied on it to survive. If they were walking along and came across a saber-tooth tiger, fear often gave them strength to fight or flee. This type of fear is useful because it protects us. The second type of fear is not really fear, but worry. It's in response to something we are afraid of, but may or may not pass. Publishing a novel that doesn't sell any copies is an imagined fear. So is the fear that your sales will stop. This fear is manufactured. While it may happen, we have no evidence of it. We mistake this fear with the ancestral fear, but it's not the same. You won't die if your book doesn't sell or if your sales dry up.

Stop being afraid of things that you imagine. Instead, be truly afraid of the things *immediately in your environment* that threaten your life.

The third cause is personal circumstances. You won't be able to write when life strikes. Deal with the problem that arises and return to writing when it is safely behind you.

BEAST #7: OVERWHELM

This staircase was long, but it led us to a black room. Obsidian floors and walls, black ceiling with only a single light in it. Good thing we brought our dragons with us since there were no windows for them to exit.

The door has shut behind us. It is locked. Our next beast isn't wasting any time!

The walls are rumbling now. They're moving in. Smoke is funneling through the walls. Soon it will be harder to breathe.

See that red button in the wall on the other side of the room? We need to push it. It seems so impossibly far away. Let's go.

Each step we take signifies action, fellow writer! But alas, we won't make it, even if our dragons push on the walls for us. The smoke...it's getting thicker and thicker...the beast is laughing just beyond the walls.

We aren't going to make it. Fellow writer, it was a pleasure knowing you. Let us lie down and accept our fate...and yes, I'm winking at you...close your eyes, my friend.

. . .

AN UNSPECIFIED AMOUNT OF TIME LATER

Ahhh, that was an amazing rest. After all these battles, it was a treat to have a nap!

Don't look at me like that. We've just destroyed the beast, fellow writer. The walls are retreating and the smoke is clearing.

The room is back to its original configuration. We'll see our opponent in three, two—a hole in the ceiling has opened and a human-like husk has fallen into the center of the room. Its limbs curl upon itself and there are no eyes.

Behold the carcass of overwhelm.

This beast wanted us to struggle. It wanted us to rail against the room with every ounce of our being. Had we done that, we would have died of our own accord, for the walls and smoke can't kill us.

When you're in overwhelm's clutches, you destroy yourself. Rest and focused action is the cure.

A staircase has appeared over there. Onward!

A MEDITATION FOR OVERWHELM

The walls will close in.

You'll feel like you can't breathe.

Your first instinct will be to fight, to tame the overwhelm. But that's the worst thing you can do.

Fighting is nothing without strategy.

You're overwhelmed because you didn't plan properly or because life just happened. You're overwhelmed because you need rest. You're overwhelmed because you're not planning properly to escape from it. In any case, the overwhelm is likely to stay with you for a while and you may not eliminate it as quickly as you like. Pace yourself and focus on one step at a time.

BEAST #8: THE GANG OF TROLLS

Fellow writer, I hope you're ready for a brawl. This staircase brings us into stone chamber with torches on the walls lighting the way. The gentle firelight and crackling fire is fodder for a battle if you ask me. I smell a whiff of something else—something rotten and decomposing.

Did you hear that, fellow writer? It sounded like footsteps.

There are eyes in the darkened perimeter of the room. They are approaching. We're surrounded on all sides.

We're up against trolls, fellow writer. Green-skinned, pot-bellied, barefooted monstrosities who need serious dental work. They're grinning, beating their clubs against their palms. They want blood.

We'll fight them, but we have to be strategic. The trolls want all-out war, but that will spell our death.

We'll drink our magic potions first. Bottoms up!

JUMPING FORWARD IN TIME

. . .

Your body freezes and you float outside of it. You, Michael, and the trolls are stuck in time.

Your vision surges forward, and you see yourself and Michael fight the trolls in fast-forward motion.

Each sword slash emboldens the trolls, making them glow red with rage. They smash you with their clubs, and before long, you and Michael both succumb. You look away as they give you both a death blow...then they hang you on the wall and admire your dead bodies.

The vision fades as you fly backward in time and re-enter your body.

BACK TO THE MOMENT

Fellow writer, our magic potion has shown us that fighting these beasts is futile. Every blow will only enrage them and make them more powerful.

Therefore, we'll play defense and use the knowledge that we learned against them. We can and will alter our destinies tonight. Shields up!

The shields are working. Roll to the side and let's weaponize our foolish trolls.

POW!

One of the trolls just knocked its friends unconscious with a club. That's the way to handle it, fellow writer. Trolls are no match for knowledge—we know their ways, don't we?

POW! Another troll down! Now we're down to a more manageable gang.

Fellow writer, look out behind you!

Damn it...we were too busy fighting that we didn't see that tentacle in the darkness. Fear has got hold of you! It's pulling you into a hole in the wall.

. . .

RENDEZVOUS WITH FEAR

You can't see anything. You slam against a wall several times as you fall downward. A tentacle is clenched around your waist.

You slash and slash, but you can't connect.

The tentacle slams you against the wall again. You seize an opportunity and slice clean through it. Somewhere far, far below, you hear a familiar scream.

You land on a dark floor. Something scurries past you.

Sensing light behind you, you run toward it and burst back into the trolls' chamber, where Michael is on the floor with his shield up as two trolls raise their clubs at him.

You draw your sword and yell to catch the trolls' attention.

AND THEN THERE WERE TWO

Fellow writer, roll out of the way. Phew! You really saved me!

POW! Another troll has fallen.

Now we're down to one lonely fellow. We'll regroup and show him the power of our swords.

He's running away, crawling through the same hole that fear dragged you into.

Good riddance, scum!

Solid work, fellow writer. Thank goodness for our potion, or we would have perished in this chamber.

I didn't expect fear to intervene, but I'm not surprised. It wants to settle the score. We'll have to keep a better lookout. Let's get out of here before that troll returns with more friends.

. . .

A MEDITATION FOR TROLLS

Trolls want to hurt you because they are hurt. The only way for them to feel better is to lash out at people they perceive to be weaker than themselves. This doesn't heal the troll; it only drives them further toward self-destruction. By destroying you, they destroy themselves, which is what they ultimately want because they're so poor at coping with their lackluster existence.

Their favorite technique is to corner you and intimidate you. They can be quite intimidating.

They want you to attack them. You're outnumbered and you'll run out of energy quickly, making yourself a quick kill for them.

The best thing to do is *not* to fight back. In the grand scheme of life, they don't matter and they know it. Their trick is to distort reality so badly that you can't think past them. They want you to fear them.

When you ignore them, they'll find someone else to terrorize.

Trolls aren't loyal to each other, so they'll eventually destroy their own too.

Better them than you.

BEASTS #9-10: MISINFORMATION AND DISINFORMATION

Fellow writer, we've come to a stone labyrinth. Who knows how many twists and turns await us. The gray stone walls rise too far for us to peek at the maze from above.

We have no choice but forward, so we'll hope for the best.

Here comes a knight, fellow writer. She looks frustrated.

"There is no point continuing. I have spent hours in this labyrinth and cannot find my way. You're unlikely to succeed either."

We'll ask her what she has seen.

"Just walls. There's no way out of this labyrinth. Stop wasting your time. Before I came here, I noticed a ledge outside that I should have used as a shortcut. I'll be using that to get around this beast. You're welcome to follow me if you like."

We'll decline her invitation. I don't remember seeing a ledge, and even if I did, our goal is to confront these beasts, not avoid them.

"Good luck, knights."

She disappears down the stairs. Let's move forward and tackle the labyrinth, fellow writer.

. . .

SEVERAL HOURS LATER...

It's hard to know if we're making progress, fellow writer, but we'll keep charging onward, for we'll eventually come to the exit.

Here comes another knight. He's running toward us and constantly looking back over his shoulder. He is afraid of something.

"Turn back!"

We'll ask him what he's afraid of.

"The beast is nearby," the knight says. "It's running toward us."

The ground is shaking, indeed. Something must be approaching us. We'll join forces with the knight and defeat the beast.

"It's a distup. They are invincible beasts. They have the heads of rhinos and weigh thousands of pounds. It is better to run."

No, fellow writer. It is better to fight. Perhaps this "distup" is the only thing between us and the exit. We may be getting closer.

The knight is fleeing. He's another casualty of the tower.

I see the shadow of a rhino's ahead against the distant wall. The beast is upon us!

It's...it's...it's...is this a joke?

Why, it's just an imp with a rhino head on a stick! It must be creating the shaking with an aural illusion. The imp is laughing at us now.

Good job putting the imp out of its misery, fellow writer. I would have been far more ruthless. Let's keep going.

. . .

SEVERAL HOURS LATER…

There's a window overlooking the stormy sea. Thick black bars won't let us escape, but perhaps it is a positive sign.

What? You see the staircase? Ha! We did it!

Look out the window, fellow writer, there is our female knight from earlier. She's climbing up onto the window sill. She has a distraught look on her face.

"No! There wasn't supposed to be bars over this window! Help me. Let me in!"

What should we say to her, fellow writer? Oh, you're cruel.

"Good luck is all you can say to me, you bastards? I thought the tip I heard was perfect for escaping the labyrinth. The ledge ends at this window and I'll have to climb my way back and then attempt the labyrinth again. What's your secret?"

Should we tell her? Very well.

"You persisted and found your own way? How does that help me?"

Let us shrug and keep moving, fellow writer. Our fellow knight has her own predicament to solve.

"Wait for me. Maybe you can guide me verbally through the labyrinth. I'll try it again. I'll—aaaaaaaaah!"

Oh, my. The window sill crumbled and our knight is plunging into the sea. Her body is flashing—it appears she wasn't a knight. She was an imp in disguise. Good riddance!

Onward, fellow writer.

A MEDITATION FOR MISINFORMATION AND DISINFORMATION

. . .

There are three types of advice in this world: advice that's meant for you, advice that's not meant for you, and advice you're not ready for yet.

The modern world is a labyrinth that's hard to navigate. We don't know whether we're making a right or a wrong turn, or whether we're proceeding or backtracking. It's easy to rely on the advice of others as a shortcut.

People give advice with good intentions, but that same advice can be so bad for us.

First, we have to worry about misinformation—advice that doesn't apply to your situation, or advice that is ill-informed in some way. For writers, misinformation leads frequently to disappointing sales. Every writer has heard about a "killer strategy" that could potentially take them full-time. It's tempting to implement that advice wholesale, but only to our detriment.

Next, we have to worry about disinformation, which is information given by people who do not have our best interests at heart. Disinformation conjures up images of shady government propaganda and politicians, but disinformation is more common than that. Look no further than "marketing entrepreneurs" on the Internet, spreading half-truths such as "you've got to try really hard to be successful" or "if you're not successful, it's your fault." They say these things not because they are true, but as a sales tactic to scare you into buying a product or somehow benefitting the marketer financially. These half-truths are a sad reality of the Internet, and the modern writer must learn to navigate them.

What happens when you fall prey to misinformation and disinformation?

When you suffer from misinformation, it ends in disappointment. You follow a marketing strategy that fails miserably for you. You can usually shake off misinformation and learn from the experience.

Disinformation is more sinister. If an action leads to shame or humiliation, you've been disinformed. Paying hard-earned money for products that have less value than you expected, or donating your time and energy to a cause that betrays its goals are good examples. To suffer from disinformation is to suffer from a malaise that you won't be able to shake for the rest of your life. It will harm you in some way and probably make you more cynical, and that's sad.

The best way to avoid both of these beasts is to focus on finding your own way. Sometimes, "doing it the hard way" is the best way. Only rely on people you can trust when looking for knowledge shortcuts. Everyone has to make a living on the Internet, but with time, you'll be able to tell when someone is giving advice from a good place versus someone trying to monetize you. There is a difference.

BEASTS #11-12: HUBRIS AND SELFLESSNESS

This staircase leads us outside and around the tower.

We've reached a balcony and our next challenge.

A fat, green blob with lazy eyes and a giant mouth sits on the edge of the balcony. To call this blob "gigantic" is an understatement.

It doesn't even know we've arrived. It's talking constantly.

"I am the best. No one is better than me. My books will be adored by the world. When this is over, I will be the most loved writer on the planet. Everyone will bow down to my power. I am going to be so rich and powerful, no one will ever doubt me again. I can do whatever I want. Any book I touch will become a bestseller. These fools may not appreciate my talent today, but soon they'll be begging for my attention. Should I entertain them? Yes, maybe I should just to see the looks on their faces. I'll make them do silly things to prove their respect for me. I am the best..."

This beast is hard to listen to. It's loud too. It's not dangerous. It's too self-absorbed to know what's happening in its environment.

The beast is opening its mouth.

There's a small speck hovering around the beast's mouth. Is that...a blob with little wings? If we listen closely, we can hear it speaking.

"I am a nobody. I am an unknown writer and no one will buy books from an unknown. Therefore, I'll just give my books away. Or I'll underprice my work. My time isn't that valuable, so I'll just give it away to anyone who asks. After all, it won't matter. I am a nobody..."

The big beast just swallowed the little beast.

Another little blob is hovering near the big blob.

The big blob is feasting on the little ones. It grows slightly bigger with every meal. Look underneath, fellow writer—the balcony is unstable and beginning to crack. It's only a matter of time before the big beast falls into the sea. And then what will happen to the little ones? They'll be lost and probably fall into the sea too.

Let's go. There's nothing else to see here.

A MEDITATION FOR HUBRIS AND SELFLESSNESS

All writers have an ego. Every person's ego is different, but all egos have one thing in common: they want to be loved.

Publishing a book means that we seek recognition.

Some people want it all. They think they are the next mega bestseller when their skills are nowhere near that level. Worse, they don't want to do the work required to level up. These writers lack humility and are incapable of empathy. They are doomed to watch the movie in their heads over and over. When others don't recognize their "brilliance," they destroy those relationships in their life, playing the victim and blaming the world for their own shortcomings. When these writers *do* write a successful book, they become horrific monsters because they believe they *deserve* their success. They'll use that to put others down. These types of writers will even turn on their readers. They are not loyal to anyone but themselves, and they cause a great deal of suffering in the world. These types are also attracted to fraudulent and unethical ideas. Laws and boundaries mean nothing to them.

All writers are also driven by a degree of selflessness. It takes a great deal of time and energy to sit in a room and make stuff up, often with no reward. Writers write to give the world stories because the world gave them stories. It's easy to be self-less and noble in this regard, but those emotions can be destructive and prevent you from making money and being more successful. It also makes you susceptible to fraud, particularly from individuals with big egos who have no empathy and will exploit your selflessness for their own personal gain.

We all hold strains of each within ourselves. Most fall somewhere in the middle.

Whenever you feel your ego inflating, temper it with humility. We all take on projects that we think will be successful but don't do well at all. That should be humbling.

Whenever you feel yourself sacrificing your time, money, or energy, ask yourself if it's worth it. It may be, but remember that readers are willing to compensate you for your writing if you let them.

BEAST #13: DESPERATION

The staircase has brought us into a tall room with stone walls.

There are large, circular holes in the walls, and two square metal grates on the left and right walls. There is an alcove at the top of the far wall, and a human-like orange sprite is dancing in it. That is our next beast. It is giving a pixie-like laugh.

Water is rushing from the holes in the wall, fellow writer. At this rate, the room will be full in a few minutes.

Do you smell that? Smoke is funneling into the room from holes in the ceiling. This smoke is making me light-headed. We won't be able to tread water if we're light-headed.

Fellow writer, the water is rising. I'm struggling to keep my bearings. That damned beast is laughing as it suffocates and drowns us! If only there were a way to get to it. See if you can throw your sword at it. Aim well!

You miss. Your sword lands in the alcove If only we could get up there!

The water is unbearable now. Fellow writer, open your eyes! Don't let the smoke get to you. We must summon our...

. . .

DESPERATE TIMES

Something pulls Michael under the surface of the water. The beast dances in its alcove, a dazzle of flames and pixie-like laughter.

Your vision is spinning in all directions. You're flailing your arms and legs wildly. The smoke is inhibiting your thinking. You're swimming for the wall, even though you don't know why. You're screaming.

A name.

You're screaming a name. Dragons?

Dragons!

You cry their names just before something seizes on your leg and drags you under the water. You barely catch your breath before you see a long purple tentacle wrapped around your leg.

You reach for your sword but remember that it's up above in the alcove. You beat the tentacle with your shield, but you lose your grip and watch as the shield floats to the floor.

The tentacle slams you against the wall. You're just a flailing rag doll now.

You grab the potion on your belt and try to put it to your lips, but the tentacle knows what you're doing. It slams you against the wall again, and you watch as the potion drops to the floor.

You think positive thoughts as the tentacle drags you through the water. It's playing with you now. You don't have any breath left.

The tentacle drags you deeper as you exhale your last pocket of oxygen. You feel a rush of energy and resist the tentacle. You feel as if you can beat it now—nothing can stop you!

And then you realize that the moment is fleeting as you blow your last bubbles.

WHAT IT MEANS TO DIE

You wake up. You're lying on a granite slate. A warm breeze makes you rise.

You're wearing a white gown. Your armor and weapons are gone. A sheer curtain brushes against your face. You behold an open window and a countryside drenched with golden light. Rolling hills are covered with pearly-white sheep. Picturesque cottages dot the landscape as if they were painted on.

You feel a hand on your shoulder.

It's Michael. He's wearing a white gown too. He's smiling.

"We fought the good fight, fellow writer. While we were no match for that beast, we have written words to show for it, and for that, we should be proud."

Michael sits down at a small wooden table. There is tea for two.

"We have no restrictions now in the land of heaven," he says. "No beasts will trouble us here. Imagine all the books we'll be able to write now without being weighed down by fear and desperation!"

A frown creeps across his face.

"We succumbed to desperation," he says. "I don't know what else we could have done differently."

You feel anger rising in your chest. How could he give up so easily? You yell at him.

"Fellow writer, I understand you're upset. But there's nothing we can do now. We are dead. Accept it and you'll move into the next phase of existence."

You ask how he could be so fine with death.

"Death is just another state of existence," he says. "Every writer dies. No one controls when their time will be. I've made peace with it. My only regret is that we died fighting desperation. That's not how I wanted to die. We had so much more to live for, didn't we, fellow writer? We were at least halfway up the tower, weren't we? That damned, damned beast...Alas. Let's drink tea and be happy, shall we?"

Michael rises the tea cup to his lips, but you smack it away.

"You're still in the throes of desperation," he says. "Maybe it'll wear off of you soon. In the meantime, let me enjoy my tea, damn it!"

A knock startles you. The door opens and a dozen people crowd into the small hut.

Michael rises.

It's a group of writers—six of Michael's all-time favorites, and six of yours. They welcome you with open arms.

You hug them and shake hands. Here you are, talking to your favorite dead writers. Who ever thought this was possible? What do you say?

One of them invites you outside. They're throwing a welcome party for you, and every writer in the history of the world will be there with gifts and kind words about your work. You are overwhelmed with joy.

For the first time since you've arrived, your death no longer stings.

As you walk outside into the pasture, each of the writers tell you their stories about the beast that killed them.

"Everyone dies from a beast," the writer says. "It's just a matter of which one. Fraud killed me. Someone stole my copyrights, and it broke my heart."

"I went into bankruptcy and my inner writer died that day," another says.

"I, too, died from desperation," another says. "I didn't know how to manage a declining writing career. I died of a heart attack, but it was brought on by anxiety related to my writing."

"I died peacefully in my sleep," one writer says. Everyone stops and looks at him angrily. The writer grins and says, "But I only wrote one book and I forever wondered what would have been if I would have slain the beast of perfection."

Everyone laughs.

"A beast claims everyone," a final writer says. "It's just a matter of which one."

In the distance, a crowd is gathered on one of the hills. They are clapping and cheering. They're standing behind a finish line and a giant banner that says "Welcome Home."

You and Michael look at each other, then you race for the finish line. Everyone cheers louder.

"I'll beat you," Michael says.

You respond with *over my dead body—literally*, and Michael laughs.

You're almost to the finish line. Just before you make it, two jagged holes appear in the air, stopping both of you.

"What the hell is that?" Michael asks.

A giant claw flies out of the hole and grabs Michael, seizing him around his waist. He screams as it drags him into the jagged hole.

Another claw grabs you, and the last thing you see is the faces of all the writers waving goodbye.

THE RETURNERS

A rush of air fills your lungs and you gasp.

You're on the back of your dragon as it skims over the surface of the water.

Two purple tentacles float lifelessly on the water, severed into pieces.

Michael is on his dragon, flying right next to you. He's as disoriented as you.

The dragons are flying upward. Suddenly, you hear a frantic scream.

The beast. In the alcove. Your sword lying next to it.

Your dragon roars, and it throws you at the alcove with its tail. You land next to your sword.

With all your strength, you grab your sword and drive it into the center of the beast's flaming body. It erupts into a column of water that splashes onto the floor and spills into the room.

The walls shake, and the water subsides, draining as rapidly as it filled. Among several pools on the floor lay your and Michael's weapons, shields, and potions.

The dragons deliver you to your weapons and you fall off into a pile of water.

You and Michael lie, catching your breath.

SAD TO BE...ALIVE?

We did it, fellow writer. But I must confess that I feel extreme sadness right now. What amazing conversations we could have had with the writers of the past!

Thank you, dragons, for saving us from sure death. That was one hell of a near-death experience.

Fear and desperation tag-teamed us. We were lucky.

We're alive now, and that's what matters at the moment. The lessons our writers in heaven taught us are not lost on me, and they shouldn't be lost on you either. Onward to the staircase that just appeared in the wall over there.

. . .

A MEDITATION FOR DESPERATION

Desperation kills. It doesn't kill you literally, but it kills certain aspects of your life if you let it.

Desperation strikes in one key area of the writing life.

When you don't see sales after several books, it can be easy to feel desperate and put all of your energy into the next book as a "final shot." If the book doesn't do well, your career is over. That's what you tell yourself. You might be down to the last hundred your spouse is willing to let you spend. Or you might think that no one will read your book if they didn't read the last five.

This act leads you to desperation, which drives you to poor decisions. You may:

- Slash your expenses and pay for suboptimal cover designers or editors.
- Stop paying for services you need, like email marketing service providers.
- Spend *too much* money in areas like marketing because you think it's your final chance.

The "final chance" mentality is an illusion. While you may face constraints in publishing, there's nothing stopping you from writing. Nothing. Writing is 100 percent free. In your mind, the "final chance" mentality can be suffocating. From the outside, you'll look to others as if you're drowning because of the self-immolating decisions you're making. A desperate writer is impossible to save.

Recognize the "final chance" mentality for what it is and try to find ways around it. If you believe you are in your final chance because of money, find ways to make more money that do not involve writing. Take on side jobs, sell things you no longer use, or stop eating out at restaurants, for example. If writing is truly important to you, you'll find a way, though it may be painful.

If you believe you are in your final chance because of advice you heard, then ignore it. It will wreck your career and lead to death.

Every writer feels desperation early in their career. And without exception, desperation kills everyone. It takes being "killed" by desperation once to realize that it's a fake death. There can be no death to the "writing" part of being a writer. Constraints only exist for a time before situations change. Everyone goes through hard economic times. Everyone goes through hard mental health times. But for most, they are temporary.

If writing is truly a priority in your life, you'll find a way around desperation.

BEAST #14: FRAUD

We come now into a pitch-black room, fellow writer.

I can't see anything. Sword ready and expect anything. I hesitate to move forward in case there is a hole in the floor or something, but we don't have a choice. We'll take small steps just in case.

Something is hissing in the darkness. I can't tell what it is, where it is, or how big it is. I have failed you—I should have armed you with a light source. I'll remember this from now on.

Something is stalking around the room. Claws on stone. A hiss.

Shields up. We'll stand back-to-back as we maneuver this room.

Look out!

A giant cat-like beast appears out of the darkness with claws drawn. I deflect it with my shield. It disappears. Look for the sapphire-colored eyes in the shadows!

Do you see that light, fellow writer? The inside of our armor is glowing now. The positive words etched into the scales are casting a faint light across the floor.

The beast comes again!

Great job, fellow writer. You slash one of its legs off. It is stalking away from us as it whimpers. Our swords will be our best friends—if we know where to slash them.

Another beast leaps at me—slash! Now it retreats.

We are being hunted by multiple beasts, fellow writer. We'll continue our trek through the darkness.

SLASH! I've slayed a beast. It just breathed its final breath.

To your left!

You've killed another one.

Let's keep moving.

I think I see a staircase in the faint light of our armor. Yes, we've arrived the staircase out of the room.

Fellow writer, the staircase is glowing now, and light is washing over the room. It's a plain room. I thought there were traps on the floor, but it's just an empty room, with a half a dozen beasts lying dead on the floor.

There are two more. Giant black cat-like beasts with glowing eyes. They seem surprised that the room is lit now. They're running away.

We're safe now. Onward!

A MEDITATION FOR FRAUD

Life is darkness, and fraud is a beast in the shadows waiting to strike when you least expect it.

Fraud comes in two forms: as a murdering shadow that strikes when you're most vulnerable, and as disinformation. Sometimes they work together.

The key to fighting fraud is understanding when you are personally vulnerable.

Some writers are insecure and doubt their ability to write

well; these writers will pay fraudsters thousands of dollars to make them feel good about their writing.

Some writers are lousy at marketing; they pay marketers and publicists thousands of dollars to market a book that won't sell.

Some writers are desperate for Hollywood contracts; they sign their copyrights away to vultures who promise everything but don't deliver.

Every writer has personal triggers that activate fear, hubris, selflessness, or desperation.

Once exploited, these triggers serve as anesthesia. Fraud will sneak in after other beasts have done the hard work. It doesn't have a strong work ethic. Fraud is the final act in a multi-beast battle. By the time it arrives, you're in too weakened a state to resist it.

To deter fraud, you must do three things.

First, improve your knowledge base. You can't succumb to fraud (or disinformation) if you're informed.

Second, establish credibility. Fraudsters are less likely to attack writers with many books and a sizable audience. These people will expose the fraudster for who they are. As someone famously said, sunlight is the best disinfectant. Fraud prefers to live in the shadows. Learn frequently, write more books and put up a professional front, and you'll deter most fraud.

Third, ward off other beasts. Fraud is a one-two punch. Much like shady contractors who ride in after a hurricane promising quick and easy repairs, fraud will also enter your life on the coattails of a separate disaster.

BEAST #15: PRODIGALITY

We come now into a room where the walls, floors, and ceiling are made of gold. How extravagant!

A throne sits in the middle of the room, and a knight sits upon it.

I recognize him. This is the same knight we encountered in our battle with the inferiority complex beast. We did the fool a favor and he resented us for it. Now he wears a crown.

"Welcome, knights!"

He's jovial all of a sudden.

"It is a good thing I didn't fight you when you deprived me of my kill earlier. Now you can see how successful I've become. Feast your eyes on my domain! Ah ha ha ha ahahahahaha..."

Not all that is gold glitters, fellow knight.

"What more do I need when I have everything I can want? Allow me to make you comfortable."

Golden chairs appear next to him.

The knight is snapping his fingers. A giant table with amazing food awaits us. It smells so good...but we'll resist.

"My food isn't good enough for you?"

The knight snaps again. Beautiful men and women

surround us. They are only wearing bathrobes—not any more. Resist them, fellow writer.

"Is it books you want?"

A pile of books with our names on them have appeared next to the throne.

"Ghostwritten for your pleasure! That still won't please you?"

A computer with hundreds of app icons appears.

"You own every app a writer can ever dream of, and that isn't enough? You truly are fools!"

Fellow writer, don't make it too obvious, but look at the walls. The gold is cracking and fading.

"I'll give you personal assistants!"

Two secretaries appear next to us. They ask us what we desire.

"You have all the time in the world! And you reject me?"

Whack!

A chunk of gold peels off the wall and crashes to the floor, exposing dull, bare stone.

"Aaaaaagh!"

The knight is screaming. He has drawn his sword. He's trying to stand up, but he can't get off the throne.

The throne's back is growing eyes and a mouth. The mouth is contorting into an evil grin. *Keep spending*, it says.

"I'll give you money!"

Coins and currency bills rain from the ceiling. Resist, fellow writer.

"What more do you want?"

A staircase has appeared behind the knight. Let's make our way toward it. The knight has stopped paying attention to us. He is trying to get off the throne but it has fused with his back. The throne is laughing all the while. The room is collapsing—let us keep moving and turn away as our friend meets his unfortunate demise.

. . .

A MEDITATION FOR PRODIGALITY

Prodigality is an underrated beast. It begins as a whisper that appeals to our innermost desire to show outward success. It tells us that we can show others how successful we've become through extravagance.

Because society intrinsically believes that writers have little value, we want to show people how much value we have, in terms society understands. It never ends well, for the world will crumble around you, and people will eventually discover you aren't as extravagant as you told them you were. Shame and humiliation remain.

Alternatively, prodigality can also accompany bad business sense. Novices writers don't budget and spend money without strategy, which leads to wasted expenses. Budgeting and understanding concepts like cash flow and return on investment (ROI) will solve this problem.

BEASTS #16-17: SUCCESS AND FAILURE

This tower is a place of wonders—the staircase has brought us into a cavernous room—rock walls, stalactites dangling from the ceiling. A flock of bats nests on the ceiling. We'll try not to disturb them. Smoke hangs in the air. I can taste a hint of fire on it. Something's burning nearby.

Seven o'clock, fellow writer! Two giant four-legged beasts are charging us. Spikes run down their backs. They growl at us through three rows of jagged, triangular teeth. Fire burns in their throats; I can smell the smoke on their breaths.

It's time for a flat-out brawl.

Wait…

The beasts are turning on each other. We were never their target. They're attacking each other now, grappling each other like fighting dogs.

A word is carved on each beast's back—"success" and "failure."

Success has failure's neck in its jaws. Failure escapes and rolls away. It's bleeding badly.

We can fight both beasts or we can wage war on the strongest and fight the remaining one.

You want to fight failure, fellow writer? Your instinct is understandable, but—

SLASH!

You dealt a deadly blow to failure, fellow writer. I'll have to join you now.

There!

With several deadly stabs, failure breaths its last breath, and it shatters to dust.

Now we have to deal with success.

The beast laughs at us. Its body is glowing now.

Get down, fellow writer!

Success has morphed to several times its size! It is spitting fireballs at us. Shields up!

This fire burns hot—our shields won't protect us forever. Our dragons won't helpful, and neither will the potion. We have no choice but to fight with our swords.

Keep slashing and defending, fellow writer, and I'll do the same.

We're weakening it some. The beast just knocked against a stalactite…

Distract it, fellow writer—I have an idea!

BATTLE WITH SUCCESS

Michael disappears into the darkness of the cavern, leaving you alone with the beast. To your surprise, the beast speaks to you.

"You chose wrong, knight. But it's exactly what I'd expect you to do. If you had killed me, you would have had an easy victory, for failure wouldn't have morphed. But how were you to know that I am the real beast in this lair?"

The beast headbutts the wall, knocking a portion of it

away. You see the bodies of many fallen knights as the beast roars with laughter.

In the corner of your eye, you see Michael climbing up another wall. What the heck is he doing? He motions you to move toward the back wall. Reluctantly, you agree as the beast stomps after you.

"Lie down and perhaps I'll spare you and kill your friend."

The beast charges you, but you slash it on the face and it recoils. It spits a fireball at you, but you raise your shield just in time.

You follow Michael's instructions and move backward as the beast stalks toward you.

Then Michael motions you toward him and you break into a mad dash as the beast follows you.

You run under Michael as he jumps into the air above you, slashing a stalactite. The icicle-shaped rock hurtles down toward the beast like a javelin from heaven and spears it in the back.

Success roars as blood splatters in all directions.

Michael lands next to you. You look at each other, and then you charge, slashing relentlessly.

DEBRIEF

Well done, fellow writer. Those beasts were tricky, indeed. We fell for their trap, but we came out with the advantage.

If only you had listened to me. I could smell the trap. Success is a far bigger foe than failure. I'd argue that success destroys more careers than failure, but that's just a guess on my part. Let's get out of here.

.   .   .

A MEDITATION FOR FAILURE

Failure is a better teacher than success. Between the two, writers are more familiar with it. They prefer to see it die quickly so they can achieve their goals.

But failure never goes away. We can defeat it, but only for a time.

Many failures is how we develop wisdom. Instead of trying to eliminate it, we should instead learn from it.

A MEDITATION FOR SUCCESS

Success is a deceptive beast. Of all the beasts, no one would suspect that success would be on the list. That's how deadly it is.

Writers believe that once they tame failure that success is the promised land. They think that money, fame, and awards are their tickets to the good life. They're surprised when they discover that success brings with it dangerous problems—namely financial problems, trust issues with relationships in their life, contractual problems, and more.

Early success is perhaps the most deadly beast of all because writers haven't had time to identify their flaws and address them. The success only magnifies those flaws and covers them with a sheen of hubris. Worse off are the writers who think their success is deserved.

The best way to battle success is to prepare for it. Plan what you would do if your business changed for the better tomorrow. Seek therapy. Watching success morph into a giant monster is traumatic. You'll never be the same after it happens.

BEASTS #18-19: PERFECTIONISM AND SLOPPINESS

We're entering a room full of straw. Straw?

Two beasts with wings are nesting on opposite ends of the room. They look like pterodactyls with human-like, blood-veined faces and bloodshot eyes. Each has a word written on their wings: perfectionism and sloppiness.

The beasts are screeching at each other. They're paying us no mind, but we won't be able to pass through the room until they're both dead.

Before you charge off and start attacking, let's think for a moment. We've seen this movie before, and we know how it ends, don't we?

Perfectionism is an unkind beast who can never be satisfied.

Sloppiness is an arrogant beast who is never good enough, and therefore wallows in jealousy and despair.

Tell me, fellow writer: if you could choose either to be your master, who would you choose? The spiked whip of perfectionism or the bottomless pit of sloppiness?

It's a terrible choice, really. I'm sure you agree. I don't know that I would choose either of them. As I told a cafeteria lady one time as a child when forced to choose mystery meat or soggy corn dogs, I'll take death instead!

Let's summon our dragons and dispense of these beasts. They're so absorbed in their quarrel that they still haven't noticed we've arrived!

Dragons, dragons thank you for coming so quickly. The floor is covered in straw. Set it on fire!

The room is engulfed in flames now. Let's back into the doorway and watch it burn.

The beasts still don't know what's going on. They're burning now. Cover your ears.

They're not even resisting the flames. They screech at each other even in death. Good riddance.

A staircase has appeared. Onward, fellow writer.

A MEDITATION FOR PERFECTIONISM

Perfectionism is poison. Once you're stuck with its barb, it'll take many years to flush the poison from your system.

Perfectionism demands your very best. It demands all of your time, attention, energy, and money. Even if you run out of all of those, it will demand more. Perfectionism can never be satisfied. If you listen to it, you will suffer from self-doubt and low self-esteem. You will forever be overly sensitive to what others think about you and your work. You will always think work is "never finished." Furthermore, you will adulterate your work and dilute it with all that time, energy, effort, and money.

The antidote to perfectionism is to develop an interior timer. Push work out before you're ready. Do a good job, but remember the law of diminishing returns. It takes years to learn how to address the poison that colors your life. You won't be perfect at it, but treat each new book as an opportunity to rid yourself of perfectionism.

Some writers wear perfectionism like a badge, not understanding that it's actually a parasite in disguise.

A MEDITATION FOR SLOPPINESS

Sloppiness is a state of mind that is difficult to escape from once you slip into it.

Most writers succumb to perfectionism. Others succumb to sloppiness. They barrel their way through books, not caring for grammar, story, or production value. They are keenly *unaware* of the fact that their skill level is mediocre. If they are aware, they do nothing to improve it. This state is like wading in your own filth, realizing it, and doing nothing about it because you think there's nothing you can do about it.

Ridding yourself of sloppiness means to clean up every aspect of your writing life and commit to quality *without* committing to perfectionism. Finding the middle ground is the key.

Develop an appetite for production cleanliness. Anything less produces mistakes that will be displeasing to your readers. Accept that you have room for improvement in many areas of your writing life, dedicate yourself to learning as much as you can, and improve incrementally over time.

For example, it's okay if your book covers aren't very good in the beginning of your career. Keep learning. It's okay if your first stories aren't perfect. Keep writing, keep improving, and learn from how readers respond to your books.

No one expects perfection, but they dislike sloppiness on sight. Perfection is the reason that so many authors never publish their books and therefore deprive the world of their stories; sloppiness is what contributes to self-published writers having a bad reputation. Avoid both beasts and you'll find yourself with easier and more reasonable expectations to manage.

BEAST #20: THE LEGAL BEAST

Fellow writer, be quiet. We come now to a giant stone chamber with a ferocious beast before us. It is the size of ten horses stacked on each other, with four salivating mouths, ten arms, and legs covered in spikes.

It sits before a giant typewriter, typing at a rapid pace. An endless page is wrapped around the room. It's a contract. This beast is writing a beastly contract with beastly terms. Every few hundred lines or so, it is ripping the paper and sending it out the window. The paper flies over the sea as if aimed. What ghastly screams these legal demand letters will elicit when received!

It doesn't see us, and let's try to keep it that way. If we have to face it, we could suffer instant death. It is the most super-charged of all the beasts we've encountered before.

Let us sneak carefully, fellow writer. The stairway over there is visible. I'm all for fighting, but this is one beast that will murder us, stop for a moment to regard our bodies, and then resume typing as if we never entered.

We've made it. We'll move quietly up the stairs, and when we're out of earshot, we'll run like hell, fellow writer!

. . .

A MEDITATION FOR LEGAL WOES

The legal beast is waiting to be activated. It sits in a stone tower waiting for you to make a legal mishap. The moment it sniffs your transgression, it will destroy you. No one has the money to afford protracted legal battles.

This is a beast you may never be able to slay, nor do you want to even try. Stay out of its line of sight. As long as you don't give it a reason to attack you, it will bother some other poor soul.

Read any contract you sign carefully and negotiate what you don't like.

Don't libel or slander people.

Read all terms of service for any services you use.

Learn the basics of the legal system in your country.

Avoid legal fights at all costs if you can.

These things will keep the beast away.

BEAST #21: THE FINAL BATTLE - SELF-DOUBT

Fellow writer, it feels like an eternity since we've entered the tower. We are just one staircase away from the top of the tower!

We've conquered the entire tower. It has been my greatest honor to fight alongside you. I cannot thank you enough for helping me redeem my legacy. Since that stormy night when I was thrown into the sea and washed away, I have kept replaying my mistakes in my mind. I've woken up in the middle of the night in cold sweats thinking about my failure. And now I have a second chance. We will take the tower together.

I should warn you about what's to come—about the beast that nearly killed me last time.

We're up against self-doubt. It is the most dangerous of all beasts, which is why it is fitting that it resides at the top of the tower.

If you've ever told yourself you can't do something, that's self-doubt talking. It catches you off-guard and then fools you into thinking that you're reasoning about yourself when you're actually doing yourself harm.

Self-doubt has many faces—self-esteem, comparisonitis, jealously, envy, self-harm, and self-hatred are all faces of this beast. Its appearance is something out of the Book of Revelation. It wouldn't surprise me if tentacles of fear accompanied the beast in battle. Self-doubt will call upon any beasts that are still living to help it.

Back on that fateful day, I was outnumbered by beasts. At least now I know I'll have backup!

Are you prepared, fellow writer? There's no turning back now. Ironically, the thunderstorms have stopped and the clouds are parting to reveal golden brown sun rays. Our battle will have a heavenly glow.

Swords ready. Shields up. Our dragons are now behind us.

Let's do this, fellow writer.

Wait, what's that sound? Behind us—it's a tentacle. How come we never saw it?! I—aaaaagh!

Slash!

The tentacle has been cut in half—thank you!

But...!

Fellow writer, I have been stabbed with a poisonous arrow. It has pierced my armor. The tentacle aimed for you, but I jumped in front of it just in time.

I...can feel venom surging through my body. Nothing will stop me. I must fight. I must...

I must sit down for a moment.

The venom is burning my veins. This pain! Oh, it's terrible!

Fellow writer, I have met my end. The venom of self-doubt runs through me. I am not strong enough to help you now.

You say that's self-doubt talking?

Ha! Maybe. But one thing is clear: I was a fool to think I could assist you and also redeem myself.

Help me sit by the window. I would like to see the sun as I drift away...

I'll be in great company. I've already seen the great beyond.

Those writers are waiting for me at the finish line. My time in eternity will be glorious, fellow writer.

But promise me something—I don't want to see you there. I'd prefer that you die a peaceful death.

Wipe away your tears. Fight to avenge me.

Let's discuss the final meditation before I lose strength...

A MEDITATION FOR SELF-DOUBT

The great invisible enemy. No beast you face will be more powerful than self-doubt. It is a force multiplier whose presence makes all other negative emotions stronger and more resilient.

If you doubt yourself, you doubt everything.

The only way through self-doubt is to have faith. You must fight and question every negative thought.

This world is full of self-doubters. In doubting themselves, they do harm to others as well as themselves.

Your goal should be to avoid harm—harm to yourself and harm to others. Self-doubt dies in the intense heat of self-love. It may strange seem to love yourself, but chances are you haven't learned how to do that. Self-doubt fills the space where love has yet to burn.

You may think you can conquer self-doubt, but it is the great regenerator—it will strike at your moments of highest confidence. It will cast you from your tower of personal power, forcing you to climb it all over again.

You must ask: who am I? Why do I write? How can I love myself better? How can I push this beast out of my life once and for all? Every day will be a battle, but you'll conquer your tower one day.

. . .

THE FINAL BATTLE

Michael passed while you read the final meditation. He sits in front of the window, sunlight bathing him in an almost holy light. You close his eyes and weep over his body.

You take his notebook with meditations. You promise to treat them well and remember everything he taught you.

A final staircase awaits you. Several sinister voices call your name. Self-doubt is waiting.

You wrap your fingers around the hilt of your sword and remember your weapons:

- A sword powered by the written word,
- armor powered by positive thinking,
- a shield powered by knowledge,
- a magic potion powered with the perspective of time,
- a dragon powered by resourcefulness, and
- a book of meditations to help you when you need the emotional support.

You have everything you need. How many writers rise to the top of this tower? So few. You saw what happened to many of them.

There's nothing to be afraid of now. All that's left is to conquer the last beast.

You charge up the final staircase to the tower roof where a fearsome roar awaits.

THE END.

READ NEXT: THE INDIE AUTHOR BESTIARY II

YOUR GUIDE TO SLAYING THE BEASTS OF THE WRITING WORLD, PART 2!

When we think we've won the battle against the "beasts" of the writing world, more appear.

The Indie Author Bestiary I taught you how to win the war against yourself. Part 2 will teach you how to thrive in a world that doesn't always understand or appreciate writers.

Learn how to:
- Banish **uncertainty** from your life
- Avoid **bad advice**
- Defeat the **stigma** of being a writer (especially an indie)
- And more!

If you struggle with the "emotional" part of being a writer, The Indie Author Bestiary II will be your armor as you climb the ladder of success.

This unique series continues the tradition of taking the emotional challenges of writing, converting them into monsters, and teaching you how to defeat them.

Are you ready to conquer the beasts of the writing world?

Get your copy today at www.authorlevelup.com/bestiary2.

MEET M.L. RONN

Science fiction and fantasy on the wild side!

M.L. Ronn (Michael La Ronn) is the author of many science fiction and fantasy novels including *The Good Necromancer, Android X,* and *The Last Dragon Lord* series.

In 2012, a life-threatening illness made him realize that storytelling was his #1 passion. He's devoted his life to writing ever since, making up whatever story makes him fall out of his chair laughing the hardest. Every day.

Learn more about Michael
www.authorlevelup.com (for writers)
www.michaellaronn.com (fiction)

MORE BOOKS BY M.L. RONN

Books for Writers

Indie Author Confidential (Series)
    How to Write Your First Novel
    Be a Writing Machine
    Mental Models for Writers
    The Indie Writer's Encyclopedia
    The Indie Author Atlas
    The Indie Author Bestiary
    The Reader's Bill of Rights
    The Self-Publishing Compendium
    150 Self-Publishing Questions Answered
    Authors, Steal This Book
    The Indie Author Strategy Guide
    How to Dictate a Book
    Advanced Author Editing
    Keep Your Books Selling
    The Author Estate Handbook
    The Author Heir Handbook

Interactive Fiction: How to Engage Readers and Push the Boundaries of Story Telling
Indie Poet Rock Star
Indie Poet Formatting
2016 Indie Author State of the Union

More Books for Writers:

www.authorlevelup.com/books

Fiction:

www.michaellaronn.com/books

APPENDIX: MEDITATIONS FOR EACH BEAST

A MEDITATION FOR FEAR

Fighting fear means to do battle with a vicious beast in a coliseum where no one is watching.

To battle fear is to battle in the darkness. No one will know you're fighting it, and no one will care.

Fear is a many-tentacled creature who will meddle in every area of your writing life. Fear is anti-creativity and loves to see you give up on your stories. It is anti-production and loves to see you revise your books to oblivion and never even publish them. It is also anti-business and anti-marketing, sowing seeds of doubt that will make you question everything.

When you confront fear, you inform it that you know its ways. This makes the beast more dangerous, for it will try to drown you in your own doubt. It will wait patiently until you die in the darkness, and then it will devour you to make sure you're gone.

Fear is the only beast who knows you better than you know yourself. It was with you from the moment you were born, like a parasitic bacteria waiting for a moment to announce its presence.

It has been with you every day of your life, and it will be with you every day in the future. It never dies; only evolves. You can never kill fear; to kill fear is to kill yourself. But you must learn to live with it.

Learn to sense those pangs of doubt. The beast has learned to sow doubt in a way that is self-soothing.

"I can't..."

"I'll never..."

"No one will..."

These are the words of fear. The moment you think them and act upon them, you'll backslide.

Stay vigilant and be ruthless to the beast. Don't reason with it; force is the only language it understands.

A MEDITATION FOR THE INFERIORITY COMPLEX

I am adequate. I am enough.

No one makes me feel inferior without my consent.

Just because the things I create may not have immediate value doesn't mean *I* don't have value.

There are things in this world that others do better than me, but that doesn't mean they are *better* than me.

I am the way I am because I prefer to be hard on myself, but kind to others.

The writing life makes me vulnerable to my emotions, but I vow to control them because it is the only thing standing between me and the control of my life.

The inferior complex has no hold on me. I will not reside in its wallowing.

A MEDITATION FOR IMPOSTER SYNDROME

In the martial art of jujutsu, the goal is to disarm your opponent by using their own force against them. You should take the same approach with imposter syndrome.

This beast makes you feel as if you are in a room of mirrors. You think that you must find the correct version of the illusion, the version of yourself that will fit in with social circles, write better, and make you happier, but it is a sham.

Resist the initial urge to destroy your imposter or minimize its power. That is what the imposter wants. It wants you to break your hall of mirrors. In doing so, you harm yourself while the imposter goes unpunished.

The imposter is not in the room. The imposter *is* the room, and it seeks to suffocate everyone in it. If you feel like an imposter, chances are that everyone in the room also feels the same way.

The easier way to destroy your imposter is to leave the room. When you do, the beast will die, deprived of its food source.

In the end, you will find that the imposter was not an imposter at all, but a snapshot of your true self, which is never an easy thing to see. But your true self belongs in this world, and it fits in everywhere you go.

A MEDITATION FOR TRAUMA

Trauma is something that happened to you, not something that is happening currently.

Fighting trauma is not intuitive. It is easier to run, yet the more you run, the more power it has over you.

Experiencing trauma initially is like being poisoned in small doses. The more you run, the more potent the poison becomes. One day, it builds up enough in your system that your body reacts negatively. It never ends well.

Therefore, your best action is to face trauma. Speak to it in the shaded darkness of your mind. It won't show its face to you, and it will scream and yell for you to go away. But when you confront it, it is powerless. It will die easily.

A MEDITATION FOR BURNOUT

Burnout is a beast that challenges us to the most high-stakes race of all time. It loves to ride, ride, ride.

We feel as if we must return the mood in kind, and so we race.

But you can never beat burnout because the racetrack is rigged in its favor. It pushes you to ride faster and faster, even though it knows you'll never win. All it takes is one mistake to explode into flames or fly off the racetrack. That's exactly what burnout wants.

To play the game, understand your instinct to achieve. That in and of itself is a good thing, but when you find yourself ratcheting up your speed, remember to slow down, for there are holes in the racetrack, and when you hit one, you will cause misery and pain for yourself.

Burnout is the feeling that you can't move yourself to write. Writing suddenly has no joy. It feels like a burden. It pains you to think about it. This is a feeling that no writer should ever have to experience, and it is preventable.

Always write what motivates you. Don't do anything you don't want to do. Have fun. Always let burnout win the race. What do you truly lose if society laps you a few times? It'll have a phony race trophy, but you'll have your dignity and a long-term author career.

A MEDITATION FOR WRITER'S BLOCK

Writer's block has three root causes.

The first cause is lack of inspiration. When you sit down at the keyboard and the words won't come, it may be because you need to fill your creative well. Reading often, consuming other media such as movies and television, and exposing yourself to new places, people, and perspectives will solve this problem in the short- and long-term.

The second cause is fear. We fall prey to the movies in our head about why we can't achieve our goals. The only way to beat fear is to keep moving forward and challenge the assumptions you hold about yourself. If you hear yourself say that you can't write a book because it's too hard, write the book anyway. You may be surprised at what happens. If you write the book, fear will retreat. If you fail, at least you tried. Fear is often always wrong.

Writers are so scared of fear. It dissuades us from doing many good things in our lives. But the secret to fear is that there are two types of fear. The first type of fear is ancestral fear; it's the warning bells that sound whenever you're in the presence of real danger. Our ancestors relied on it to survive. If they were walking along and came across a saber-tooth tiger, fear often gave them strength to fight or flee. This type of fear is useful because it protects us. The second type of fear is not really fear, but worry. It's in response to something we are afraid of, but may or may not pass. Publishing a novel that doesn't sell any copies is an imagined fear. So is the fear that your sales will stop. This fear is manufactured. While it may happen, we have no evidence of it. We mistake this fear with the ancestral fear, but it's not the same. You won't die if your book doesn't sell or if your sales dry up.

Stop being afraid of things that you imagine. Instead, be truly afraid of the things *immediately in your environment* that threaten your life.

The third cause is personal circumstances. You won't be able to write when life strikes. Deal with the problem that arises and return to writing when it is safely behind you.

A MEDITATION FOR OVERWHELM

The walls will close in.

You'll feel like you can't breathe.

Your first instinct will be to fight, to tame the overwhelm. But that's the worst thing you can do.

Fighting is nothing without strategy.

You're overwhelmed because you didn't plan properly or because life just happened. You're overwhelmed because you need rest. You're overwhelmed because you're not planning properly to escape from it. In any case, the overwhelm is likely to stay with you for a while and you may not eliminate it as quickly as you like. Pace yourself and focus on one step at a time.

A MEDITATION FOR TROLLS

Trolls want to hurt you because they are hurt. The only way for them to feel better is to lash out at people they perceive to be weaker than themselves. This doesn't heal the troll; it only drives them further toward self-destruction. By destroying you, they destroy themselves, which is what they ultimately want because they're so poor at coping with their lackluster existence.

Their favorite technique is to corner you and intimidate you. They can be quite intimidating.

They want you to attack them. You're outnumbered and you'll run out of energy quickly, making yourself a quick kill for them.

The best thing to do is *not* to fight back. In the grand scheme of life, they don't matter and they know it. Their trick is to distort reality so badly that you can't think past them. They want you to fear them.

When you ignore them, they'll find someone else to

terrorize.

Trolls aren't loyal to each other, so they'll eventually destroy their own too.

Better them than you.

A MEDITATION FOR MISINFORMATION AND DISINFORMATION

There are three types of advice in this world: advice that's meant for you, advice that's not meant for you, and advice you're not ready for yet.

The modern world is a labyrinth that's hard to navigate. We don't know whether we're making a right or a wrong turn, or whether we're proceeding or backtracking. It's easy to rely on the advice of others as a shortcut.

People give advice with good intentions, but that same advice can be so bad for us.

First, we have to worry about misinformation—advice that doesn't apply to your situation, or advice that is ill-informed in some way. For writers, misinformation leads frequently to disappointing sales. Every writer has heard about a "killer strategy" that could potentially take them full-time. It's tempting to implement that advice wholesale, but only to our detriment.

Next, we have to worry about disinformation, which is information given by people who do not have our best interests at heart. Disinformation conjures up images of shady government propaganda and politicians, but disinformation is more common than that. Look no further than "marketing entrepreneurs" on the Internet, spreading half-truths such as "you've got to try really hard to be successful" or "if you're not successful, it's your fault." They say these things not because they are true, but as a sales tactic to scare you into buying a product or somehow benefitting the marketer financially. These half-truths are a sad reality of the Internet, and the modern writer must learn to navigate them.

What happens when you fall prey to misinformation and disinformation?

When you suffer from misinformation, it ends in disappointment. You follow a marketing strategy that fails miserably for you. You can usually shake off misinformation and learn from the experience.

Disinformation is more sinister. If an action leads to shame or humiliation, you've been disinformed. Paying hard-earned money for products that have less value than you expected, or donating your time and energy to a cause that betrays its goals are good examples. To suffer from disinformation is to suffer from a malaise that you won't be able to shake for the rest of your life. It will harm you in some way and probably make you more cynical, and that's sad.

The best way to avoid both of these beasts is to focus on finding your own way. Sometimes, "doing it the hard way" is the best way. Only rely on people you can trust when looking for knowledge shortcuts. Everyone has to make a living on the Internet, but with time, you'll be able to tell when someone is giving advice from a good place versus someone trying to monetize you. There is a difference.

A MEDITATION FOR HUBRIS AND SELFLESSNESS

All writers have an ego. Every person's ego is different, but all egos have one thing in common: they want to be loved.

Publishing a book means that we seek recognition.

Some people want it all. They think they are the next mega bestseller when their skills are nowhere near that level. Worse, they don't want to do the work required to level up. These writers lack humility and are incapable of empathy. They are doomed to watch the movie in their heads over and over.

When others don't recognize their "brilliance," they destroy those relationships in their life, playing the victim and blaming the world for their own shortcomings. When these writers *do* write a successful book, they become horrific monsters because they believe they *deserve* their success. They'll use that to put others down. These types of writers will even turn on their readers. They are not loyal to anyone but themselves, and they cause a great deal of suffering in the world. These types are also attracted to fraudulent and unethical ideas. Laws and boundaries mean nothing to them.

All writers are also driven by a degree of selflessness. It takes a great deal of time and energy to sit in a room and make stuff up, often with no reward. Writers write to give the world stories because the world gave them stories. It's easy to be self-less and noble in this regard, but those emotions can be destructive and prevent you from making money and being more successful. It also makes you susceptible to fraud, particularly from individuals with big egos who have no empathy and will exploit your selflessness for their own personal gain.

We all hold strains of each within ourselves. Most fall somewhere in the middle.

Whenever you feel your ego inflating, temper it with humility. We all take on projects that we think will be successful but don't do well at all. That should be humbling.

Whenever you feel yourself sacrificing your time, money, or energy, ask yourself if it's worth it. It may be, but remember that readers are willing to compensate you for your writing if you let them.

A MEDITATION FOR DESPERATION

Desperation kills. It doesn't kill you literally, but it kills certain aspects of your life if you let it.

Desperation strikes in one key area of the writing life.

When you don't see sales after several books, it can be easy to feel desperate and put all of your energy into the next book as a "final shot." If the book doesn't do well, your career is over. That's what you tell yourself. You might be down to the last hundred your spouse is willing to let you spend. Or you might think that no one will read your book if they didn't read the last five.

This act leads you to desperation, which drives you to poor decisions. You may:

- Slash your expenses and pay for suboptimal cover designers or editors.
- Stop paying for services you need, like email marketing service providers.
- Spend *too much* money in areas like marketing because you think it's your final chance.

The "final chance" mentality is an illusion. While you may face constraints in publishing, there's nothing stopping you from writing. Nothing. Writing is 100 percent free. In your mind, the "final chance" mentality can be suffocating. From the outside, you'll look to others as if you're drowning because of the self-immolating decisions you're making. A desperate writer is impossible to save.

Recognize the "final chance" mentality for what it is and try to find ways around it. If you believe you are in your final chance because of money, find ways to make more money that do not involve writing. Take on side jobs, sell things you no longer use, or stop eating out at restaurants, for example. If writing is truly important to you, you'll find a way, though it may be painful.

If you believe you are in your final chance because of advice you heard, then ignore it. It will wreck your career and lead to death.

Every writer feels desperation early in their career. And without exception, desperation kills everyone. It takes being "killed" by desperation once to realize that it's a fake death. There can be no death to the "writing" part of being a writer. Constraints only exist for a time before situations change. Everyone goes through hard economic times. Everyone goes through hard mental health times. But for most, they are temporary.

If writing is truly a priority in your life, you'll find a way around desperation.

A MEDITATION FOR FRAUD

Life is darkness, and fraud is a beast in the shadows waiting to strike when you least expect it.

Fraud comes in two forms: as a murdering shadow that strikes when you're most vulnerable, and as disinformation. Sometimes they work together.

The key to fighting fraud is understanding when you are personally vulnerable.

Some writers are insecure and doubt their ability to write well; these writers will pay fraudsters thousands of dollars to make them feel good about their writing.

Some writers are lousy at marketing; they pay marketers and publicists thousands of dollars to market a book that won't sell.

Some writers are desperate for Hollywood contracts; they sign their copyrights away to vultures who promise everything but don't deliver.

Every writer has personal triggers that activate fear, hubris, selflessness, or desperation.

Once exploited, these triggers serve as anesthesia. Fraud will sneak in after other beasts have done the hard work. It doesn't have a strong work ethic. Fraud is the final act in a multi-beast battle. By the time it arrives, you're in too weakened a state to resist it.

To deter fraud, you must do three things.

First, improve your knowledge base. You can't succumb to fraud (or disinformation) if you're informed.

Second, establish credibility. Fraudsters are less likely to attack writers with many books and a sizable audience. These people will expose the fraudster for who they are. As someone famously said, sunlight is the best disinfectant. Fraud prefers to live in the shadows. Learn frequently, write more books and put up a professional front, and you'll deter most fraud.

Third, ward off other beasts. Fraud is a one-two punch. Much like shady contractors who ride in after a hurricane promising quick and easy repairs, fraud will also enter your life on the coattails of a separate disaster.

A MEDITATION FOR PRODIGALITY

Prodigality is an underrated beast. It begins as a whisper that appeals to our innermost desire to show outward success. It tells us that we can show others how successful we've become through extravagance.

Because society intrinsically believes that writers have little value, we want to show people how much value we have, in terms society understands. It never ends well, for the world will crumble around you, and people will eventually discover you aren't as extravagant as you told them you were. Shame and humiliation remain.

Alternatively, prodigality can also accompany bad business sense. Novices writers don't budget and spend money without strategy, which leads to wasted expenses. Budgeting and understanding concepts like cash flow and return on investment (ROI) will solve this problem.

A MEDITATION FOR FAILURE

Failure is a better teacher than success. Between the two, writers are more familiar with it. They prefer to see it die quickly so they can achieve their goals.

But failure never goes away. We can defeat it, but only for a time.

Many failures is how we develop wisdom. Instead of trying to eliminate it, we should instead learn from it.

A MEDITATION FOR SUCCESS

Success is a deceptive beast. Of all the beasts, no one would suspect that success would be on the list. That's how deadly it is.

Writers believe that once they tame failure that success is the promised land. They think that money, fame, and awards are their tickets to the good life. They're surprised when they discover that success brings with it dangerous problems— namely financial problems, trust issues with relationships in their life, contractual problems, and more.

Early success is perhaps the most deadly beast of all because writers haven't had time to identify their flaws and address them. The success only magnifies those flaws and covers them with a sheen of hubris. Worse off are the writers who think their success is deserved.

The best way to battle success is to prepare for it. Plan what you would do if your business changed for the better tomorrow. Seek therapy. Watching success morph into a giant monster is traumatic. You'll never be the same after it happens.

A MEDITATION FOR PERFECTIONISM

Perfectionism is poison. Once you're stuck with its barb, it'll take many years to flush the poison from your system.

Perfectionism demands your very best. It demands all of your time, attention, energy, and money. Even if you run out of all of those, it will demand more. Perfectionism can never be satisfied. If you listen to it, you will suffer from self-doubt and low self-esteem. You will forever be overly sensitive to what others think about you and your work. You will always think work is "never finished." Furthermore, you will adulterate your work and dilute it with all that time, energy, effort, and money.

The antidote to perfectionism is to develop an interior timer. Push work out before you're ready. Do a good job, but remember the law of diminishing returns. It takes years to learn how to address the poison that colors your life. You won't be perfect at it, but treat each new book as an opportunity to rid yourself of perfectionism.

Some writers wear perfectionism like a badge, not understanding that it's actually a parasite in disguise.

A MEDITATION FOR SLOPPINESS

Sloppiness is a state of mind that is difficult to escape from once you slip into it.

Most writers succumb to perfectionism. Others succumb to sloppiness. They barrel their way through books, not caring for grammar, story, or production value. They are keenly *unaware* of the fact that their skill level is mediocre. If they are aware, they do nothing to improve it. This state is like wading in your own filth, realizing it, and doing nothing about it because you think there's nothing you can do about it.

Ridding yourself of sloppiness means to clean up every aspect of your writing life and commit to quality *without* committing to perfectionism. Finding the middle ground is the key.

Develop an appetite for production cleanliness. Anything less produces mistakes that will be displeasing to your readers. Accept that you have room for improvement in many areas of your writing life, dedicate yourself to learning as much as you can, and improve incrementally over time.

For example, it's okay if your book covers aren't very good in the beginning of your career. Keep learning. It's okay if your first stories aren't perfect. Keep writing, keep improving, and learn from how readers respond to your books.

No one expects perfection, but they dislike sloppiness on sight. Perfection is the reason that so many authors never publish their books and therefore deprive the world of their stories; sloppiness is what contributes to self-published writers having a bad reputation. Avoid both beasts and you'll find yourself with easier and more reasonable expectations to manage.

A MEDITATION FOR LEGAL WOES

The legal beast is waiting to be activated. It sits in a stone tower waiting for you to make a legal mishap. The moment it sniffs your transgression, it will destroy you. No one has the money to afford protracted legal battles.

This is a beast you may never be able to slay, nor do you want to even try. Stay out of its line of sight. As long as you don't give it a reason to attack you, it will bother some other poor soul.

Read any contract you sign carefully and negotiate what you don't like.

Don't libel or slander people.

Read all terms of service for any services you use.

Learn the basics of the legal system in your country.

Avoid legal fights at all costs if you can.

These things will keep the beast away.

A MEDITATION FOR SELF-DOUBT

The great invisible enemy. No beast you face will be more powerful than self-doubt. It is a force multiplier whose presence makes all other negative emotions stronger and more resilient.

If you doubt yourself, you doubt everything.

The only way through self-doubt is to have faith. You must fight and question every negative thought.

This world is full of self-doubters. In doubting themselves, they do harm to others as well as themselves.

Your goal should be to avoid harm—harm to yourself and harm to others. Self-doubt dies in the intense heat of self-love. It may strange seem to love yourself, but chances are you haven't learned how to do that. Self-doubt fills the space where love has yet to burn.

You may think you can conquer self-doubt, but it is the great regenerator—it will strike at your moments of highest confidence. It will cast you from your tower of personal power, forcing you to climb it all over again.

You must ask: who am I? Why do I write? How can I love myself better? How can I push this beast out of my life once and for all? Every day will be a battle, but you'll conquer your tower one day.